THE FASTEST SELLING LINE OF SPORTS CAR BOOKS EVER PUBLISHED

A series of low-cost books designed to meet the skyrocketing demand for more information on these trim, sleek, high-performance machines. Each volume, written by an expert, deals with one of the more popular makes or with some general phase of the sport. Fully illustrated, these attractive and practical manuals are designed for the thousands of owners, would-be owners, and enthusiastic devotees of rallies, races, and expert road driving.

CARE AND REPAIR OF YOUR SPORTS CAR—*Ritch*
TRIUMPH GUIDE—*Allen & Strome*
HOT AND COOL VW's—*Williamson*
ACCESSORIES FOR YOUR SPORTS CAR—*Reid*
CORVAIR GUIDE—*Tanner*
VOLKSWAGEN GUIDE—*Carroll*
SPORTS CLOTHES FOR YOUR SPORTS CAR—*Weitz*
MG SPORTS SEDAN GUIDE—*Stone*
MG GUIDE—*Christy & Ludvigsen*
STIMSON'S RALLY FACTORS
FORMULA JR.—*Morrow*
YOU CAN DRAW CARS—*Jenks*
SO YOU'RE GOING TO BUY A USED SPORTS CAR—*Stone*
FORD COBRA GUIDE—*Carroll*
THE BUGATTI STORY—*Boddy*
LARRY REID'S RALLY TABLES
GUIDE TO CORVETTE SPEED—*Ludvigsen*
HOW TO WIN AT SLALOM AND AUTOCROSS—*Pagel*

NEW JAGUAR GUIDE—*Williamson*
GUIDE TO RALLYING—*Reid*
NEW PORSCHE GUIDE—*Sloniger*
GUIDE TO COMPETITION DRIVING—*O'Shea*
SPORTS CAR CLUB—*Reuter*
TRICKS OF THE RACING TRADE—*Stiles*
FAMOUS RACING CARS—*Hodges*
HILLMAN MINX GUIDE—*Page*
AMERICAN VINTAGE CARS—*Betts*
NUVOLARI—*Count Lurani*
ALFA-ROMEO GUIDE—*Ayling*
MUSTANG GUIDE—*Stone*
SUSPENSION GUIDE—*Norbye*
MERCEDES-BENZ COMPANION—*Ullyett*
DKW GUIDE—*Ayling*
TODAY'S VW GUIDE—*Williamson*
THE NEW FIAT GUIDE—*Norbye*
THE NEW GUIDE TO RALLYING—*Reid*
RACING DRIVER'S SCHOOLS—*Stone*
STICK SHIFTER'S GLOVE BOX COMPANION—*Whitehead & Bilsland*

SPORTS CAR PRESS
Publishers of Automobile and Aircraft Books
Distributed by CROWN PUBLISHERS
419 Park Avenue South, New York, N.Y. 10016

How To Win At
SLALOM
&
AUTOCROSS

by Jim Pagel

edited by William S. Stone
photography by Jim Pagel
photography edited by John Brand

New York
SPORTS CAR PRESS

Produced by Silvermine Production from type by Darien
Phototypographers and printing by LithoCrafters.
Manufactured in The United States of America.

Library of Congress Catalog Number 70-162587
ISBN 0-87112-053-4

CONTENTS

CHAPTER I

INTRODUCTION

Since you've already gone out and spent tomorrow's lunch money on this book, you'll be wanting to know what you've got. Briefly, what it offers is a new and proven approach to winning at slaloms. Solo-car timed events are virgin territory for a smooth technique and a couple of clever but legal tricks.

If you haven't run a slalom-type event yet, it would be a good idea to go out and run one before you read any further. It's not absolutely necessary. But to fully grasp the techniques you will learn, you should get the basics first. For those of you who have already knocked down your share of pylons, read on...

To make easier reading, and to make sense, this text will be divided in three main categories: The Event, The Car, and The Driver. Each is integral in itself and can be read separately if desired. All three combined will cover everything you will have to know to not only compete and win, but also to set up, organize, and administer solo-car timed contests. Remember, there are plenty of drivers but far too few administrators. What the sport needs are active participants and organizers to build an effective, growing slalom program.

The Event section will specifically explain equipment, advertising, and administration.

The Car section covers basic set-up principles that can be applied to any type of car. Obviously, with so many types of cars running slaloms, no one book could cover them all. Each of the set-up techniques were

Slaloms can give racing thrills and speeds at a cost we can all afford — and do it with the car we drive to work every day.

Mini-Coopers are formidable opponents at a dirt hill-climb.

taken from winning cars. Any modifications that didn't help are not included. It has been narrowed down to just those few that give the most return for your money. You won't need expensive equipment to be competitive.

The Driver chapter is the last. Here is where you will find those driving and confidence-building tricks that will knock seconds off your times and line your trophy shelf. You may skip ahead and read the last chapter if you like. But you'll appreciate it more if you take it in the proper order.

A few words about the history of our sport. Early slaloms and time-trials seldom come up in conversation, but the facts may settle an argument for you at a club meeting someday.

There is little formal writing about just when early wheel-to-wheel club racers decided to set up solo-car trials against a clock instead of one another. As many books and photographs and veterans tell us, early sports car road racing was an informal Sunday afternoon picnic and "...just take the windscreen off, Ralph" affair. Their good-natured camaraderie was just about the way slaloms are today. However, as in most sports, the dealer/factory sponsored publicity seekers soon raised their expensive heads.

The little local guy usually found himself going home talking to himself with a basket full of engine parts after trying to beat the money-boys.

Drivers were faced with the decision of either going "all the way" or falling back to run the less sophisticated, friendlier, solo-car events. Many chose the latter. Road racing is not expensive solely because of money. Time is the element that most of us cannot afford. Keeping a car competitive and driving in one or two races a month is a full time job!

Race weekends are generally two-day affairs, and taking off from work on Friday is a good idea if you want to be sure of passing Tech Inspection. Cars must be cussed at, repaired, and maintained between races; which means a good two or three nights a week, till way past midnight usually, and not by yourself either.

You are going to need a crew for both weekends and those evening "wrench" sessions. Try to find a couple of amateur mechanic/engineers who are willing to volunteer 20 or 30 hours a week lying on a cold garage floor, to pay their own expenses on these 2 or 3 day out-of-town jaunts, and are willing to sacrifice social life, marriage, family, and employment. Cherish your crew when you find one, if you can.

Solo car events' popularity rose mainly in the late '50's and early '60's. The old MG's, Jaguars, early Corvettes, Triumphs and Austin-Healeys were the backbone of the "new" timed races. Owners found that they could drive their cars to work during the week and still take a trophy on Sunday. Wives and girlfriends actually enjoyed accompanying their men on the pleasant picnic-like excursions.

Slaloms have retained their informality. I've spent many, many pleasant hours in a staging line, pushing the car ahead a few feet every couple of minutes and having a friendly argument with the MGB in back of me about the fastest "line" for that tough pylon at the end of the straight.

Depending on what part of the country you live in, you will probably use roughly the following brief definitions:

Slalom — Becoming the most popular. Basically, it is a fairly high speed parking lot event in which the course usually does not cross itself and there are no backing-up or gimmick activities.

Autocross — A generally higher speed, longer course, often run on airports or large parking lots. Usually the course is fairly complex and may cross itself at some point, probably in the middle. The words "slalom" and "autocross" are often used interchangeably with little damage.

Slaloms can be an enjoyable pastime for the entire family. A father-son relationship can benefit tremendously.

Driving techniques acquired at a slalom will stay with you all your life.

Time Trial — Often held on an actual road racing course, they are some of the fastest of the solo-car series. Some events require roll-bars and competition licenses. Hill climbs may occasionally be called time-trials. Many time-trials require a competition car and license.

Hill Climbs — Popular in the more hilly regions of the country, they can be held on either public, private, paved or unpaved roads. They are the most difficult events to administer. Hill climbs require terrific organizational procedures, crowd and traffic control, and elaborate timing devices.

Gymkhanas — Are dying out. They are being phased out almost everywhere. Once a driver has had a taste of a fast course, he has little patience for hopping around his car on one foot at the start-line, balancing an egg on a spoon in his mouth.

Each of these different style events will be generally covered throughout the book. The same principles of driving apply to all these variations. The idea is always to go from point "A" to point "B" as quickly as possible.

Now slide down in your chair, pull that can of beer a little closer and get comfortable. Here we go into the more specific, meaty slalom talk...

Few thrills can equal the elation of driving a fine sports car at speed. Slaloms give you a chance to do it in safety.

AMCC AMCC AMCC AMCC AMCC

may 31st

A TRI-STATE SANCTIONED SLALOM

HEAVY DUTY

Monday, May 31, 1971

This season's highest speed slalom !!
At Capitol City Speedway, Oregon Wisconsin
It's a HEAVY 1/2 mile banked asphalt oval !!
Helmets and seat belts are mandatory.
Registration limited to 125 enteries.
Registration: 9:00 am till 11:00 am
Drivers meeting at 10:45 am
Timed runs start at 11:00 am, end about 5
Late registration is from 11:00 am till 1:00
Cars will be run by class, A stock first

COST: AMCC member pre-reg. $6.00
       NON-AMCC pre-reg. $6.50
       At track registration ALL $7.00

*Pre-registration must include form below
and check payable to AMCC and must be
post marked no later than May 25, 1971.

- -

PRE-REGISTRATION FORM

NAME: _____ ADDRESS: _____ ZIP _____

MAKE OF CAR: _____ MODEL: _____ COLOR: _____

HORSE POWER: _____ CU. IN. or CC: _____ TRI-STATE CLASS: _____

ARE YOU A TRI-STATE REGISTERED DRIVER?? _____

IS CAR, FACTORY STOCK:? _____ MODIFIED ENGINE ? _____ RACE TIRES ? _____

SEND TO: Neil E. Matthes   1001 East Meadow Place   Whitefish Bay, Wis   53217

ANY QUESTIONS ?, CALL NEIL AT 414-332-9412   OR NANCY E.   AT   414-242-0537

Typical "flyer" advertising up-coming slalom. Items contained in it can be used as model for your own "flyers".

14

CHAPTER II

THE EVENT

There is a great difference between a well-organized, efficiently-run slalom and the all-too-typical hasty affairs that seem so numerous. The difference is planning and manpower. The reputation of your club is at stake every time you stage an event. Profit should not be your sole motive.

This chapter will assist you in putting on a successful slalom. The Event section of this book is divided into Advertising, Registration, Timing & Scoring, Course & Equipment, and Safety & Tech. Even if you have only been a driver, this chapter will give you an insight into what makes an event "tick," and what to look for when you evaluate a slalom as a driver.

Advertising

Your procedure in organizing your event depends largely on the number of slaloms in your area. If your locale has had very few of these events in the past, then publicity and advertising will be your first concerns. You are going to have to get the car-driving public interested. Once you get them there and they watch for a while, hopefully their curiosity will overcome their reluctance. Most slalomists began as spectators, and some eventually return to spectating.

If slaloms are popular in your town, advertising is much easier. Often just "word-of-mouth" and the club grapevine will bring all the customers you will need. However, if there are a large number of events, you are going to have to concentrate on presenting a sophisticated, smoothly-run competition. Once your club has earned a reputation for excellent events, your future turn-out is assured.

Advertising will be your greatest asset. Naturally, you'll be printing "flyers" announcing your date, location, time, classes, etc. Print up enough copies: they're cheap. Quantities of over 1000 are often not too many. If your club does not have a slalom mailing list, make one up. Talk to the presidents of other sports car clubs in your area. Get names. Use your own club's member mailing list. After all of your events, use the names and addresses of entrants to send them announcements of your next date.

Local sports car dealers and hot rod shops are good spots to drop off a stack of flyers. Drag strips and even rallies are good distribution points. Car-nuts are universally interested in any kind of a speed event and many will turn out, even if only as spectators. Once you can get a driver to watch, it won't be long before he's itching to make a fool of himself on the course.

Newspapers are another good source. Many papers have a week-end sports activities column and are happy to print your announcements, free of charge. Many radio stations will broadcast announcements of public service, non-profit type activities. Even local TV stations have been known to transmit film taken at a slalom on the Monday evening news program. Give your TV station a call about a week in advance; you may be surprised at the results.

One of the best gimmicks for building public support is the "charity event." Find a good cause, and the media will bend over backwards to handle your publicity. Charity benefits will win you the support of local businessmen and the police support that you are going to need to find a suitable location to hold your events. Finding an appropriate open, paved parking lot has frustrated many an ambitious slalom campaign. Parking lot owners are notoriously reluctant to allow a

If you have spectator or traffic problems, a string of flags can control them.

crowd of sports car owners to "tear up" their parking lots. Property owners have everything to lose and nothing to gain. Their good will is all that you need. Once you have staged several events with no incidents or damage, the task becomes much easier.

Local municipal government can even assist you. Most cities have municipal parking lots that are not used on Sundays. Your alderman or other local official can help you. This is where the charity event idea comes through. If you use the profits from your first couple of slaloms to support a local orphanage, for instance, you will be amazed at the doors that begin to open to you.

If you haven't joined a sports car club yet, join one. You are going to need an organization behind you, even if you're not planning on sponsoring an event. If you only want to drive, club meetings and club newsletters are the best sources for future dates and locations. Most clubs have a "clique" of slalomists. Ask questions. Slalomists are a friendly bunch and they like to take an inquisitive newcomer "under their wing." They can save you a lot of frustration and mistakes.

Registration

The idea of any registration is to process the greatest number of entrants in the shortest possible time. To

Truck, van or mini-bus is the best place for timing and registration. Sides provide a "blackboard" for posting results sheets.

facilite this, you will need a minimun of two workers. Women are great for this.

At Registration, you should:

1) Receive the registration fee
2) Get the liability release form signed
3) Inform the entrant of his class
4) Give the entrant his registration number
5) Get the entrant's name and address
6) Explain the general rules and schedules for the day

If all of the above can be accomplished, the need for a "drivers' meeting" is virtually eliminated.

You will need certain articles of equipment that are basic to all slaloms:

The Milwaukee Sports Car Club uses a simple micro-switch on a tripod, with a fishing-rod tip wand at the finish line. When the finishing car hits the wand, the timer is stopped.

Electric eyes are becoming more and more popular as timer-tripping devices. They can be stationed far enough from the track so they won't be hit by an over-enthusiastic driver.

1) Release forms (on a clipboard) - to technically release the sponsors and organizers from any liability. We won't go into the legal aspects, but just let it be said that the insurance underwriters require it, so we live with it. Besides, they are also used to get the entrant's name and address on one convenient list for future mailings.
2) Envelopes - In my area, we have found it a good practice to have each entrant self-address a blank envelope that will be used to send him his re-

3) A cigar box - It may sound silly, but it's the best place to keep your money from blowing away.
4) A class list - Should be posted at registration, in an easily visible location, to show entrants where their cars are classed and to eliminate a lot of argument.
5) General rules or instruction sheet - Schedules, general rules, tech inspection instructions, staging area locations, etc., will all save you repeated questions.
6) Miscellaneous little hand-lettered signs explaining entry fees, age limits, and "have your driver's license ready, please" will speed up registration.
sults and dash plaque.

And, most important, you are going to need a suitable spot for your registrants to sit. They must be out of the sun, the rain and the wind. Nothing is more frustrating than having your papers and money blowing all over the parking lot. A station wagon or large sedan, with a suitably large "Registration" sign hanging on it, works the best. Park the vehicle away from the actual course. There is going to be a crowd milling around, so it must be in a safe area. Since you are going to need more volunteers for this job in the future, it pays to make your workers as comfortable as possible.

This inexpensive timer was built by a club member.

Timing, Scoring, & Posting

The foundation of all timed, solo-car events is accurate, objective, concise "times," clearly posted for everyone to see. If a driver cannot see how he is doing, half of the fun is gone. The idea is to beat the other guy. You can't beat him if you don't know how fast he is going, or how fast you're going.

There are two basic types of timing: electro-mechanical and hand-held stopwatch. The trend is toward the electronic techniques. They are more consistent and accurate than stopwatches. Basically, these timers are simply .001 decimal minute counters activated by two switching devices, one at the start and one at the finish. These switches can be of several different types:

1) Electric eyes - most popular. They can be positioned several feet on either side of the course, in comparative safety, and are very reliable. The light source is the critical unit. It can be from 6 to 12 volt and is usually of the car spotlight variety, although portable dry-cell type searchlights have been used. Both the eye and the light source must be mounted on an adjustable tripod so they can be aligned.

2) Micro-switches - Switches can be used, either at-

tached to a wand that strikes the car as it passed, or in a "ding-dong" type of gas station drive-over hose. Our club, the Milwaukee Sports Car Club, uses a wand (an old fishing rod tip) fastened to a heavy steel tripod. It is an inexpensive solution and seems indestructible. Many cars have hit the finish tripod over the years, with damage only to the cars and the drivers' dignity.

Here are the items you'll be needing for timing, scoring, and posting:

1) Timing device - We've already discussed these a bit. Canvass your club for an electronic engineer, and with a little friendly persuasion, he'll be happy to throw an electric-box together for you. All the parts shouldn't cost over $25.00. Of course, you can always use stopwatches. Some clubs have used two operators, each using a watch and timing simultaneously, then averaging the two readings. This never did make much sense and causes too many fist-fights between the two operators. Better to use one watch and one operator all day. This elimates the differences in reaction-time and judgement you would have between several different operators throughout the day. Have a standby operator and watch in case your number one boy faints from heat prostration.

2) Shoe polish - to mark registration numbers and classes on the sides of cars. Buy the liquid sponge-top bottle type in both black and white. You won't use black very much, but it's nice to have for those occasional white cars. Try several different brands to find one that applies nice and thick and washes off easily. Some of them are terribly hard to get off. Some clubs put numbers on both sides of the car so that the number can be seen wherever on the course the car may be. Ac-

tually, depending on your start-finish layout, one side of the car is enough. As long as all cars will be starting and finishing in opposite directions, you will be able to identify them either when they start or when they finish. If your timing station is between the start and finish with the start to the left and the finish to the right, a number on the passenger door will be visible at either the beginning or end of the course. It works better to have one person do all the marking of cars. If each driver marks his own, you get much eccentricity of letters and fancy artwork that makes them hard to read. Besides, you won't lose as many bottles of shoe polish if your workers do it. Tech inspection is the best time to mark cars.

3) Large cardboard posters - for each class. Draw these up ahead of time. Use a ruler and get your lines nice and straight. Good timing posters give an event "class." They should be large enough so each driver's times can be read from twenty feet away.

4) A "results" sheet (see example) - Draw up a results sheet with driver's name, car, and times for his 1st, 2nd, 3rd, 4th, and last runs. You will need one of these for each class. They are exact duplicates of your large timing posters. As each car moves up to the start line, you note his class (marked with shoe polish on the car), pull the proper sheet, and at the end of his run you enter his time and number under the proper column. Every 15 minutes or so, these sheets are given to another worker to be posted and then returned. Having these sheets can eliminate many arguments. Once you've drawn up the original sample, have a hundred or so copies run off, and they will last all year.

POLAR-TWO SLALOM

Class A

* 1.	Jim Pagel	Corvette	0.955
* 2.	Rick Saulig	Corvette	0.962
3.	Rick Saulig	Corvette	0.967
4.	Jim Pagel	Corvette	0.972
5.	David Hatch	914-6	1.025
6.	Randy Hoeft	Corvette	1.052
7.	John Taucher	Corvette	1.088
8.	Del Grasper	Corvette	1.103

Class B

*1.	Jim Bacon	AMX 360	0.990
*2.	Vaughn	Mimi Cooper	1.011
3.	Jim Bacon	AMX 360	1.039
4.	John Noll	Jag XKE	1.040
5.	Lawrence Luser	GT 350	1.043
6.	D. P. Alberti	AMX 390	1.055
7.	Larry Beckley	240-Z	1.090
8.	B. Zimmermann	Tiger	1.094
9.	Larry Beckley	240-Z	DNF

Class C

*1.	John Vlasis	MGB	0.960
*2.	Dick Luening	MGB	0.975
3.	Mark Eskuche	A-H 3000	0.979
4.	John Staab	MGB	0.991
5.	Dick Luening	MGB	0.993
6.	John Staab	MGB	1.005
7.	Tom Lives	A-H 3000	1.023
8.	Rick Landusky	MGB	1.049
9.	Tom Lives	A-H 3000	1.057
10.	Steve Parker	Midget 1275	1.057
11.	Tom Westcot	MGB	1.179

Class S-1

*1.	R. Wittenberger	Shelby 500	0.980
*2.	Jeff Jamrozy	Mustang 289HP	0.999
*3.	Chuck Ryan	Mustang 351	1.016
4.	R. Wittenberger	Shelby 500	1.014
5.	Roger MacGregor	AMX	1.021
6.	Roger MacGregor	AMX	1.025
7.	Ed Treis	Z-28	1.062
8.	Don Pinkalla	Camaro	1.065
9.	Ronald Davis	Camaro	1.073
10.	Dennis Soric	Camaro	1.115
11.	Lee Gaglino	T.A. Firebird	1.121

Class S-2

*1.	Peter Probst	GTO	1.007
2.	John Rastler	Camaro	1.025
3.	Ken Schmitt	BMW	1.033
4.	Tony Machi	Camaro	DNF

Class D, S-3, S-4, & S-5

*1.	Rick Retter	Mini 850	1.033
*2.	Mike Mauer	Saab	1.044
3.	Mike Mauer	Saab	1.046
4.	Graig Mills	Mid. 1100	1.066
5.	Neil Matthes	Corvair	1.077
6.	Ken Krueger	VW 1300	1.084
7.	Ed Kaufman	Sprite 940	1.177

Class A, B, & C Race

*1.	Jim Pagel	Corvette	0.890
*2.	Chauncey Martin	A-H Food	0.896
3.	Chauncey Martin	A-H Ford	0.919
4.	Dick Luening	MGB	0.931
5.	Bob Mertes	A-H Ford	0.952
6.	Gary Ohm	Chevelle	0.977

Ladies Class

*1.	Judy Zimmerlee	Sprite 1100	0.948
*2.	Nancy Matthes	Corvair	0.942
3.	Marna Matthes	Corvair	0.869
4.	L. Bruss	Sprite 1275	0.866
5.	Sue Eskuche	A-H 3000	0.844
6.	J. Fitzgerald	Sprite 1275	0.809
7.	Geri Staab	MGB	0.803

(Times are Average percentages of 2, 3, 4 placing cars in mens class.)

* Indicates Trophy Awarded

Event Chairman: Chauncey Martin

Next MSCC Event: Blackhawk High Speed Slalom May 15th, 1971
Call Jim Pagel 476-2098
Pre-registration only

Typical results sheet, with times broken down by class.

5) Masking tape and thumb tacks for hanging posters.

6) Several fiber-tip pens for marking times.

7) Naturally, a suitable location must be found to keep your timer happy. The Milwaukee Sports Car Club always tries to use a van-type truck parked between start and finish facing the course. The van supplies the 12 volts needed for the timer as well as shade and comfort for the operator.

A micro-switch finish line in action. Occasionally a car will hit the tripod, but it's never a serious mishap.

You must keep people away from the timing station. Use either pylons, ropes or barriers to isolate the position. Too many people crowd around the timer trying to find out the time for their last run or their competitor's last run.

Course And Equipment

The idea in a slalom is to offer as many variations in types of corners as you can. Variety makes it interesting. Some clubs have developed the technique of marking course lines on each side of the course. They simplify staying on course and give a sort of "road race" feeling. Chalk or lime and water mixtures are used in regular industrial "line painters."

The author feels that fewer pylons (a single one if possible) used in the right position, can mark off exactly the same course as many more. Fewer pylons allow a choice of "line" and eliminate that railroad-track feeling. Gates, especially many gates in a row, are too restrictive.

25

The need for precision driving should be present, but not to the extent that some clubs carry it.

A slalom should not be won by the driver with the best memory and sense of direction. Too many pylons just lead to confusion. A slalom chairman should realize that he has a bad course if 25 or more of the drivers DNF. (Did Not Finish.)

The next slalom you run, study the course. Notice how many pylons really serve no purpose. The same course could be marked off without using a "sea of pylons" and an army of course marshals.

A really tight course unfairly handicaps drivers in longer, wider cars. Relatively speaking the same gate in a Sprite is a lot wider than it is in a Camaro. There are often cars of greatly different size in the same class. Witness the Lotus Super Seven and Corvette. Both cars have approximately the same acceleration (small block Corvette), and yet it will take greater skill and effort

These pylons are not tall enough. Taller pylons would make the course easier for the driver to see.

on the part of the Corvette driver to be competitive, simply because the car is so much bigger.

Another good technique is to give an automatic DNF for any pylon that is knocked over. This discourages hot-footing and lessens the need to set up pylons all day. Many clubs have been giving a 3 to 5 second penalty for hitting one. Since a time penalty will kill that run anyway, competitively speaking, why not just call it a DNF and avoid a lot of mathematics, confusion and argument.

A popular rule is the "displaced pylon" theory. That is, any pylon that is touched or moved, as well as tipped over, is penalized. This is bad because it is too subjective. Too much luck is involved. The course marshal may not see a pylon get touched. Maybe it's on the other side of the car and can't be seen. Maybe the course marshal was glancing away for an instant. Slower, less dramatic cars are not observed as closely as faster, potentially fast-time-of-day cars. Most pylons fall over as easily as a "bag of groceries on your car seat" anyway. A tipped-over pylon is easy to see and usually even the driver knows about it. Let's try to avoid controversy and keep things fair for everyone.

You'll need the following items on your course:

1) Pylons - preferably bright yellow or orange. The newer plastic ones are best. Buy them at least 24" tall; 36" is even better. Usually they cost from $3.00 to $5.00 apiece. Some clubs buy two colors, say, orange and green. All orange pylons would be located on the right-hand side of the course; all green on the left-hand. This works out very well and simplifies finding the course. You'll need twenty to sixty pylons, depending on the size and sophistication of the course.

2) Chalk to mark your pylon locations - they must all be replaced on exactly the same spot after being knocked down. The course must stay the

ITEM	OK	REJECT 1	REJECT 2	COMMENTS
COCKPIT				
Safety belts, secure				
Passenger seat & back secure				
All loose objects removed				
Brake pedal pressure				
Fire extinguisher, secure				
BODY				
Trunk cleared of loose items				
Hubcaps removed				
Number properly located				
Hoods, decks, & panels secure				
Exhaust pipes & brackets				
SUSPENSION & RUNNING GEAR				
Wheel bearings				
Steering linkage				
Wheels & tires - reasonable tread (no "baldies")				
Wheel lugs tightened				
Suspension & shocks				
ENGINE COMPARTMENT				
Fuel & Oil leaks				
Wiring				
Brake fluid level				
Front brake lines (in wheel well)				
Oil & gas lines & filter caps				
Radiator & hoses				
Fan belt & generator brkts.				
Battery secure				
MISCELLANEOUS				
Helmet				
Brake Test				

OK for competition .... Date ....

name

TRI-STATE REGIS. DRIVER? Yes☐ No☐   **PLEASE PRINT** | CAR # _____

NAME _____ | CLASS _____

ADDRESS _____ | TECH _____

_____ | STATE _____
city   state   zip

PHONE # _____ DRIVERS LICENSE # _____

CAR _____
make   model   eng. disp.   color

CLUB AFFILIATION _____

How did you hear of this event? ☐ Mail ☐ Newspaper Other _____

Does your car have any of the following:

YES NO

___ ___ Race designated series or non-street warranted tires?
___ ___ Wheels or Vehicle Body of non-stock dimensions?
___ ___ Track or Wheelbase changed from stock dimensions"
___ ___ Number, make, or size of Carbs changed, or addition of Fuel Injection?
___ ___ Gutted or modified Interior, or substitution for or removal of glass?
___ ___ Intake or Exhaust Manifolding of non-stock configuration?
___ ___ Updating or backdating which would affect classification?
___ ___ Limited Slip Differential.
          For American made cars other than Corvette --
          Does your car's engine have Hydraulic Lifters ☐ or Solid Lifters ☐

Typical tech card (both sides shown).

same for all competitors, all day.

3) Rope and barricades - to block off entry and exit roads and keep the crowd in a safe location. Stray cars must be kept out of the area. All of us have seen a lost, bewildered station wagon driver in the middle of the course trying to figure out what all the dumb pylons are for and which way to the supermarket.

Remember, keep the course simple and your people will go home happy. Forget the gimmick rally jazz and keep the driving in our sport.

Safety And Tech

Slaloms have an excellent safety record. Let's keep it that way. Tech your cars to eliminate those that are obviously unsafe. Loose exhaust pipes, sloppy ball joints, bald tires, and no brakes have all been discovered in a tech line.

You will find that serious competitors are not the ones you have to worry about. They keep their vehicles in tip-top condition. The ones to really check over are the older, dilapidated jalopies whose owners have never run a slalom before. They may go home a little mad at being turned down, but that's better than going home injured or dead.

Make up a good tech card as a guide and check-off for your inspectors. At least two inspectors should check each car, one on each side. You will need two teams to process the tech line fast enough. You should tech a car in roughly sixty seconds, so that two teams can process 120 cars an hour.

Safetywise, you should have several large fire extinguishers located around the course. They can be rented if need be. Instruct several workers in their function. If possible, get a worker that has been through the SCCA's corner worker's school.

You should have at least one long pry-bar for righting overturned cars. Small sedans (especially Mini's and Fiat 850's) have a nasty habit of rolling over on

Slaloms can be a very social sport. The staging line is a good place to meet new friends.

Go-kart tracks duplicate road-racing thrills on a smaller scale. Their natural layouts reduce the need for pylons.

their backs in the middle of the course. They could catch fire. Asbestos gloves and a belt knife should be available at the start-finish line.

Naturally, all drivers are required to wear seatbelts. Your tech inspectors are responsible for checking seat-belt condition and secureness of mounting. Any driver seen not using his belt must be disqualified for the rest of the day.

Helmets are recommended for *all* cars. There has been discussion as to whether helmets are really necessary in closed sedans. They are. A large sedan, coming to an abrupt halt against a building, a light post or a concrete curb can do considerable damage to an unprotected human head.

Besides, a helmet gives kind of a "racy" feeling to a driver when he confidently puts his helmet on, carefully fastens the chin strap, and slowly, methodically slips his fingers into his imported Italian driving gloves while his girlfriend stands nearby watching, nearly overcome with admiration for her hero-driver.

Crowd control is vital. A small child wandering across the course could be disastrous. Delegate the responsibility for this to someone you can rely upon. Your crowd control man will have to keep parked cars in proper area, keep the timing area clear, and keep spectators a safe distance from the start-finish lines and the course.

Your club will have to have insurance, both liability and property damage. The cost is reasonable. You will find it will be very difficult to find a parking lot to run on without insurance.

Summary: THE EVENT
Equipment needed:

Registration — 1. Release forms
                            2. Envelopes
                            3. Cigar box
                            4. Class list

                                    5. General rules
                                    6. Misc. signs
Timing & Scoring — 1. Timer or watch
                                    2. Shoe polish
                                    3. Posters, each class
                                    4. Pack of paper
                                    5. Masking tape, tacks
                                    6. Pens

Course Equipment - 1. Pylons (20-60)
                                    2. Chalk
                                    3. Rope, barricades (or pylons)

Safety & Tech — 1. Tech forms, clipboards
                                    2. Pens
                                    3. Screwdriver, to check brake master cylinder
                                    4. Tire gauge
                                    5. Fire extinguishers
                                    6. Pry bar
                                    7. Asbestos gloves
                                    8. Knife

Your staff should be approximately:
1. Chairman of event
2. Co-chairman of event
3. Registration - two women; ½ day job
4. Timing & Scoring - one timer; one postee; one standby; all day
5. Course - one course marshal; all day
6. Tech - two 2-man teams; ½ day job
7. Crowd control - one man; all day

These are pretty minimum requirements. However, you can use your registration women for timing and scoring after registration closes. Tech inspectors can serve on other jobs after tech closes, and the co-chairman can often handle timing and posting.

A brief word should be mentioned about trophies. The different types that are awarded are staggering. They range from pewter mugs to chromium eagles standing atop a beer can with a simulated marble base. Try to keep your trophies of a high caliber. Cheap trophies make the sport look amateurish. Nobody wants a lot of Mickey Mouse statues on his mantel. Something that can be functional is well-received.

The Milwaukee Sports Car Club gives nothing but genuine pewter mugs, with a glass bottom, and engraved with event name, date, club, and placing. They can be used for decoration or drinking beer. A large number of them makes a very impressive display, even in the most distinguished surroundings. They cost only roughly $7.00 engraved, and no one has ever complained that they were cheap-looking. These mugs retail at $12.00 to $14.00 engraved at most stores.

Slaloms can be much bigger than they are at present. All we need are one or two big sponsors that recognize the spectator appeal of a 427 Cobra maneuvering through a tight course, in full view at all times. The TV coverage possibilities have been virtually ignored because nobody has ever pushed for it.

The midwest area has organized into the Tri-State Slalom Conference. Clubs in Illinois, Michigan, Wisconsin, and Indiana offer a series of championship slaloms all following the same classes and general rules with annual class champions.

California has organizations of clubs devoted to slaloms. The Pennsylvania Hillclimb Association has proved successful.

These coordinated attempts indicate the future possibilities for national championships.

As long as we maintain the integrity of the pure-stock classes, the possible influx of dealer/factory sponsored equipment will not bother the little-guy.

Slalom Schools

One of the best methods to build enthusiasm in your club is to hold a "Slalom School". These events are very simple to organize and the expense is negligible. You may even make a few dollars on it. The

Slalom schools are the only place that you'll get "on the job" training right in the car. Note instructor beside driver.

idea is to use the same type of parking-lot that you would normally stage your slaloms on. The only difference being that there are no trophies, 2 people may ride in a car, and each run is comprised of 4 complete laps around the course.

The best time of the year to hold your school is in the early spring, before the slalom season begins. Something you might try is staging the event on a Saturday before a Sunday slalom. You might even use the same parking-lot. The two events could be advertised on the same flyer and a price reduction could be worked out for drivers that attended both days.

Instructors will be needed for each of the four basic types of cars; small sedan, large sedan, small sports, and large sports. Your instructors should be the best drivers in your area. Not only to assure the best possible instruction, but also to gain your pupils' respect. A $2.00 fee should be charged to cover expenses. In return for the fee the driver receives a registration number, a course drawing, and a score sheet. Make a list of the drivers' names and addresses to add to your slalom mailing list.

Before any runs are taken, a brief class session should be held. Discuss subjects like safety, tire pressures, and starting-finishing line procedures. Make up a list of the items you want to discuss. This book can be a good reference for selecting your topics.

Next, have the class walk through the course in 4

Instructors Name _____

Registration Number _____

Drivers Name _____ **Club Affiliation** _____

Car Make _____ **Model** _____ **Color** _____ **Class** _____

This is your scoring-sheet. Give it to the timer before you take your run. Ask for your sheet back after you complete each run.

Run #1	*Run #2*	*Run #3*
Lap 1 _____	Lap 1 _____	Lap 1 _____
2 _____	2 _____	2 _____
3 _____	3 _____	3 _____
4 _____	4 _____	4 _____
Comments:	Comments:	Comments:
Run #4	*Run #5*	*Run #6*
Lap 1 _____	Lap 1 _____	Lap 1 _____
2 _____	2 _____	2 _____
3 _____	3 _____	3 _____
4 _____	4 _____	4 _____
Comments:	Comments:	Comments:

Instructors Evaluation:

Scoring sheet for use in slalom driver's school.

groups, led by their instructor. The instructor will explain proper corner "lines", braking points, and give general driving tips.

After 15 minutes or so spent familiarizing the students with the layout, your first group can begin their practice. Be sure to time these first runs because they are a good comparison point for later, faster runs. In order to time each individual lap you will need a "snap-back" style stopwatch. That is, with each depression of the top button the watch will "zero" and automatically restart. As the timed vehicle passes your point of reference (usually two pylons in line) you would note the time, hit the button, and then write the time you read from the watch on the score sheet. Each driver would receive four lap times for each of his runs. The score sheet should be given back to each driver at the completion of each run. He may be allowed to keep the sheet at the end of the day.

Lay out your course so that the standing-start on the first lap will not slow down the first lap time. Start the cars off to the side so that they will pass in front of the timer at approximately the same speed they would achieve on a normal lap.

Your instructors have several options with their students. They may ride with the student as observers, they may watch the students from any point on the course, they may drive the students' cars with the students either watching or riding along, or they may take students for drives in the instructors' car.

By giving each student back his score sheet with his four times after each run, the student is able to see if he is making any progress and can compare times with his buddies. By the end of the day, the score sheet should tell an interesting tale. Most drivers will find that they are lapping considerably faster than they were in the morning, and that their driving is much easier because they're not afraid of the course anymore.

To add a little competition, it's a good idea to have each group instructor take several laps in his own car in the morning and then post the times to show what the potential is for that type of car. It gives beginners something to shoot at. You might even find that some students are beating their instructor's times, to the embarrassment of the instructor.

Slalom schools work very well for women drivers too. Women normally are very reluctant to drive at a slalom. They are afraid that they might appear foolish, just as men are. Since the events are always solo affairs, there is little opportunity to get instruction. But at school she can drive with her husband, or boyfriend, or an instructor. There are very few women that won't enjoy a fast, safe ride with a man they trust. Even if your women students never actually begin to compete at events, at least they will be much more understanding toward their men's hobby.

Women's Class

Women have a right to complain. They have been consistently ignored by almost every Club. Slalomists never seem to realize that by seeking the favor of their wives/girlfriends, they insure their own continued participation in their favorite sport.

Most women lack the basic competitive nature of men, but they still enjoy beating other women. You are going to have to get this friendly competition started. A little good-natured kidding and ridiculing can go a long way.

A good gimmick is a special ladies' trophy, larger than the usual first-place award. It costs a few dollars more, but it will encourage husbands to persuade their wives to give it a try.

Slalom schools are another excellent method of getting reluctant females behind the wheel. Any woman feels much more confident if she can learn while sitting next to her man.

Many clubs have experienced problems in "classing"

women drivers. It's not really fair to put them in a men's class against men. They will be driving everything from a Volkswagen to a race-tired Corvette. So you can't put them all in the same ladies class on a straight-time basis.

We have found that most effective technique is to use the "percentage" principle or "time differential" scoring procedure. The idea is to rank each woman's car against the corresponding men's class for the same car. The woman that comes closest to the men's time for her type of car wins. Some clubs use only the second-place men's time for this comparison (see TRI-STATE rules at the end of this book). Other clubs use an average of the 2nd, 3rd, and 4th placing men's times. Either way usually gives the same results. You can either subtract the women's time from the men's comparison-time and get the difference or "differential" (naturally the smallest difference would win). Or you can divide the men's time by the women's time, giving a percentage (the highest percentage winning). A differential is the fastest. It saves a lot of mathematics.

Your club can greatly benefit from getting the women interested. Give it some thought. Maybe the next time you try to budget-in a set of race-tires, the "old lady" will happily forget that new washing machine she's been wanting. And what better way to improve your wife's driving?

Team/Club Challenges

If you want to ignite some real club spirit, put out a club challenge to all the other clubs in your area. Challenge them to send their best drivers, as a 5-car team, to beat your best. Nothing will bring your drivers closer, and strengthen your club more, than a Team Challenge.

The administration of a Challenge event is really quite easy. You'll need an impressive trophy for the winning team. It can be either a permanent award or a "traveling" trophy that is held by the winners until the next Challenge. The travelling version should be engraved with the winning club's name and date.

Points are awarded to each team member according to his class placement as follows:

1st....9 pts.		4th....3 pts.
2nd....6 pts.		5th....2 pts.
3rd....4 pts.		6th....1 pt.

The totals are added for each team and the most points wins.

Each team should be assessed $5.00 to cover the additional trophy costs. Each member can kick in $1.00 to his team captain to cover this.

It's a good idea to give each winning team member some kind of an award. Wall plaques, jacket patches or regular trophies could be used. Naturally, this team trophy would be in addition to the trophy he may have taken by himself.

Allow each club to enter as many teams as they can get together. Most clubs will have their "Super-Team" with all their best drivers, and maybe a second or third team with their less experienced drivers. It's hard to tell a man he's not good enough to make the team. Don't turn anyone down. Make as many teams as you can.

Your No. 2 team will drive better than they ever have before. They'll be striving to make the No. 1 team. Your No. 1 team will be fighting to hold its prestigious position. Everyone will drive better.

The secret in winning a Club Challenge is not only having the fastest drivers, but having drivers in classes they can win. Consider the competition. Stack your team in the classes that you know they can win. Sometimes you're better off with a little slower driver in a class that is not so competitive. Some of the less popular classes often only have 6 or 7 entrants. Strategy is the name of the game.

Another very successful technique is for your club to hold a series of events during the entire season, with a point competition for the year.

The Milwaukee Sportscar Club stages 7 events every year, one a month. The driver with the most points at the end of the year is awarded the large championship trophy. This point competition is open only to Club members, which helps induce people to join. The slalom series keeps drivers coming to all of your events. They can't afford to miss any championship points.

The SCCA SOLO II Series

A recent addition to our sport has been the SCCA's SOLO II Series, or slalom series, sponsored in conjunction with Schlitz beer. This is the first attempt at a Nationwide slalom program. Even though Schlitz has discontinued their support for economic reasons, the seed has been planted. The series remains healthy and growing.

The prominence and reputation of the SCCA have been an asset in securing public support. This group has always seemed to attract the upper classes of sportscar buff: the ones that drive the Cobras, Porsches, and Lotuses. Local clubs never had much appeal to these drivers. Some people have good-naturedly called it "snob appeal", but there's no denying that the SCCA has most of the truest purists around.

We are seeing more new faces than ever before and a whole new group of slalomists are emerging. Their interests had previously been restricted to Rallying and Road-racing. Some of the early SOLO II events, in my region, reflected the SCCA's lack of slalom experience. But they learned fast and the most recent events were as good as anybody's.

There is no reason why a National Slalom Run-off couldn't be held, similiar to the American Road Race of Champions held at Atlanta every year. We cannot expect sponsors or support until we achieve nationwide unity. The SCCA is the only group that is in the position to do this. Let's get with it, boys.

CHAPTER III

THE CAR

Since there are about 7,233 different types of cars that are running slaloms, obviously this book can't give specific spring rates, sway bar sizes, and wheel offsets for all of them. What it will do is to give corrective measures to the basic car handling problems in several dif-

One of the cars that began it all: the Lotus Elan. If there is one classic slalom car, the Lotus is it.

ferent categories of vehicles. They are:
1) Sedans, large; over 105 in. wheel base, including all pony cars.
2) Sedans, small; economy and sports models; in most cases, imports.
3) Sportscars, small; all imports, let's say with less than 150 HP.
4) Sportscars, large; fire-breathing honkers with over 150 HP.

A section will be devoted to each of the above four categories. The last part of this section will be devoted to general set-up tricks, advantages in race tires, street versus race cars, trailering, equipment, etc.

As certain phrases will be used repeatedly, we'll define them before we start:

A. Understeer - Condition prevalent in heavy front-engined cars; that is, the front of the car will tend to plow in a straight-ahead direction when you want it to turn. A typical condition on American sedans. The average driver is safer in an under-steering car, so Detroit builds them that way. Can be identified at a slalom by great squealing and smoking of the front tires in a sharp turn, along with the knocking down of many pylons on the outsides of turns with the *front* bumper.

B. Oversteer - Ralph Nader's neurosis. Rear-engined cars have a tendency to spin around; that is, the rear of the car wants to go faster than the front. A good driver can really make an oversteering car "dance" through the pylons. Also can be identified by the knocking down of many pylons on the outsides of turns with the *rear* bumper.

Before we generalize all the way from the sublime to the ridiculous, we'll cover each of the four types of cars briefly:

Large Sedans

With precious few exceptions, large sedans are sole-ly American-produced vehicles. They are becoming

42

Bolt-on options will transform a sedate street machine into a bellowing stormer. But remember: every heavy-duty part you add will reduce your car's street practicality.

This **AMX** demonstrates that power-induced oversteer can be a fast, if tricky, way around a corner.

one of the largest classes at slaloms. These cars can be driven to work every day, carry the kids in the back seat, and still make the owner feel sporty. Since the longer wheelbase cars like Chevy Impalas, Torinos and Chryslers are seldom seen at slaloms, we'll interpret this class as being mainly Z-28's, Boss 302's, Challengers and Javelins. These cars are the largest untapped sources of future slalomists. Most of their owners haven't the slightest idea what a solo-car timed event is. It is our job to try to introduce them.

In factory condition, most of these cars suffer from understeer. Soft suspension is the villain here. What Detroit feels is comfortable riding is not an ideal slalom suspension. We need a tightly-sprung car that can rapidly veer in different directions without rolling the tires off the rims.

The fastest, easiest way to lessen understeer is to add a rear sway bar, if you don't already have one. Detroit has taken to adding these to their most recent super-sporty cars. These bars are inexpensive, $15 - $20, and they do not appreciably affect the ride. If you are going to add one to your car, buy a factory-built model. The small accessory companies that sell sway bars charge the same prices as the factory, but the mountings are often flimsy, and they are prone to rattle and break off.

Another, more expensive, correction for understeer is heavier, lower front springs. These can help substantially. But stay away from a heavier front sway bar. This is the worst thing you can do. A heavier front bar *increases* understeer. That super-heavy 1.5 inch diameter front bar will eliminate front lean, but you'll just plow merrily right straight off the corner.

Shock absorbers will do a lot to correct lean without substantially changing the steering balance characteristics. They simply make the car quicker to respond by reducing pitch and roll. That is, they reduce the transition time of your suspension from hard-left to hard-

The Z-28's factory suspension package is both difficult and expensive to improve upon.

right by reducing suspension travel. Good stuff 50-50 shocks make the recovery much faster after a turn. Your tires will stay on the ground better, and your accelerating and braking will be more effective.

Get the best shocks you can afford. Koni's are your choice if you want the ultimate. They're expensive, roughly $100 for four, but they are worth every penny. I've never talked to a driver yet who's had Koni's that didn't swear by them.

There are replacement heavy-duty adjustable shocks on the market (priced from $12.00 to $20.00 each), but they never seem to last much more than 10,000 miles!

Get some Koni's. They're worth it in self-confidence alone.

Tire pressures can have a marvelous effect on your handling, or they can ruin it. Generally speaking, you want to increase pressures in the end of the car that you want to stick better. If your car is plowing, increase

Corvettes have all the basic equipment needed to win. All that's necessary is a few adjustments.

the front pressure 4-6 lbs., or reduce the rear pressure by the same amount. You'll always want to have at least 30-32 lbs. in the front of a sedan to lessen tire rollover. You needn't worry about a modern tubeless tire coming off the rim. This writer has inadvertently spun a Corvette, on street tires, on a road course at over 90 mph and didn't lose a pound of air. Several times, as a matter of fact!

A good starting point in a Z-28 or Firebird would run around 30 lbs. rear and 34 lbs. front. Some drivers run as high as 40 lbs. (cold) in the front, but you'll find that you are losing too much tire "footprint." The tire is only riding on the center of the tread.

This type of car is a prime candidate for the new 60 series tires. They are very low profile (25″ to 26″ diameter) and put over 8″ of rubber on the road. You will need at least a 7″ wide rim. Go to 8″ if your club rules allow it. Steel Corvette wheels in the 15″ × 8″ size will fit Camaros and Firebirds. They can be purchased for only $15 to $18 each and are the best buys on the market.

46

Another good technique to overcome understeer and to balance out handling is to run a lower profile tire on the front. Say, E-60's on the front and G-60's on the rear. They lower the front roll center and give faster steering response.

B.F. Goodrich's new Radial TA 60 Series has proved to be the best combination street and slalom tire. They give excellent wear and superior adhesion. These tires seem to get better and better as the tread wears down. New ones are a little slippery until you scuff them in, as are most tires. Confine your tire choices to the major brands: Firestone, Goodyear or B.F. Goodrich. There are many, many hot-rod specialty tires with wide treads and a "hairy" pattern, but they never seem to handle well on a slalom course. Their deep, aggressive tread pattern is too unstable. Sort of like a snow tire. They get their traction by virtue of their extremely soft rubber compounds, which doesn't help tire-life any.

If you go to a wider wheel, stick with the factory wheels. Most of the hot-rod "mags" have greater offset than a stock wheel. All of the increased width is to the outside, greatly increasing the burden on your wheel bearings, spindles and fender lips. Before you buy that set of 15″ × 8″ wheels, verify that your slalom rules allow it. Some cars are restricted to 14″ wheels because the factory never offered 15″ wheels as an option. Usually the auto manufacturers have wheels in a 14″ × 7″ size with a stock offset available through dealers.

It is difficult to convince drivers what a tremendous difference good front-end alignment will make. For slaloms, you want from 3°-4° positive caster and 3°-4° negative camber. The caster causes the tire to be strongly self-centering; that is, the steering wheel will spin back to center when you release it after a turn, which will reduce your manipulating time considerably. It will make turning the wheel a bit harder, but

Notice the negative camber on the front of this Mustang. Some drivers run as much as 4 or 5 degrees.

it is well worth it.

Negative camber plants your tire flatter on the ground in a turn and gives the car a better "stance." Amazing how fast you can blast through a series of pylons by just turning the wheel into the corner, releasing it, and hitting the gas pedal. The car seems to straighten out automatically when you release the wheel.

Horsepower is nice if you've got it, but don't spend a lot of money to get it. Slaloms are won by a high *average* speed. You can do it much easier by simply having a better handling car in the turns. The fastest sedan in my area is a 302 inch Camaro with a two-barrel carb and an automatic transmission. What he lacks in acceleration, he makes up in handling. This stormer runs Koni shocks and B.F. Goodrich TA's. The two-barrel carb is strong on low-end torque, and the automatic's torque multiplication complements it.

The usual hot-cammed street-racer type cars don't begin to turn on till over 4000 rpm. That's too late in a slalom. Get yourself an engine/transmission/rear end ratio combination that pulls peak torque in the 20 to

50 mph. ranges. Stay away from the large block engines. The 396, 427, 390 class of engines just don't work for most drivers. Torque is nice, but only in reasonable quantities. The big-block engines also add an additional 150 lbs. on your front wheels, which is just exactly where you don't want it.

Seriously, you will very, very seldom see an equally-well-driven large-block engined car beat a similar type of car with a medium-sized mill (302 to 350 cu. in.).

There have been millions of words written on getting horsepower from all types of engines. Get yourself a good dyno tune-up, to include modifying your distributor's advance curve and re-jetting your carburetor. This will get you 75% of the horsepower that you'd get with unlimited cash! Leave it at that.

Let's set up a mythical sedan to win at slaloms. We'll talk Camaro, because you can virtually duplicate the specs in either a Javelin, Firebird or Mustang.

From your dealer you would order:

1) 4 speed transmission; wide-ratio (about 2.52 first gear), which gives a good low 1st, 2nd and 3rd, but still allows cruising on the highway.
2) 3.55 Positraction (approx.) rear end with the above wide-ratio transmission.
3) Variable-ratio power steering; or fastest ratio manual steering. There are arguments for and against power steering - you decide. This writer prefers manual.
4) Heavy-duty suspension (includes rear sway-bar) and widest wheels.
5) Power disc brakes.
6) Engine in the 350 cu. in. area with a four-barrel.
7) 60 series tires (B.F. Goodrich TA's if you can get them).

The above car will give reasonable gas mileage and you can drive it to work everyday. After you take delivery of our mythical dreamboat, you should make the following additions:

To the chagrin of Porsche owners, Corvairs have demonstrated remarkable handling qualities.

1) Small foam-padded flat steering wheel, about 14″ diameter.
2) Koni shocks, all around (or any good H.D. 50-50 shock).
3) Rear traction bars.
4) A good dyno tune-up and minor engine mods.
5) Front alignment at 3° negative camber, 4° positive caster and ⅛″ toe.

With the above combination, you will be ready to run in a stock class and give a good account of yourself at any slalom in the country.

If you heed the above suggestions, you'd better get yourself a bigger trophy shelf, because you will *have* the proper equipment.

Imported Sedans

We'll discuss imported sedans in two broad categories: sporty-type sedans like BMW, Alfa, Saab, etc; and the economy-type like VW and Renault.

The newer Pinto, Vega, and Gremlin can be in either of the two classes. You can get options to make them perform either as "handlers" or as "cheapies."

The imported sporty models handle about as well as you'll ever be able to make them. The only options available to these cars are factory competition parts that are notoriously hard to get and darn expensive. One or two of these racing parts won't make that much difference. The competition equipment is designed to be part of a complete package. Putting a Weber carburetor on a Volkswagen will not make it a race car!

Cars like the Datsun have complete books of factory racing components that dealers will get for you. But remember, every one of these parts that you add reduces the value of your car as everyday transportation. In effect, with all the racing stuff, you'll end up with a car that you either won't want to, or won't be able to, drive everyday. Rather than spend this much for parts, if a race car is what you want, buy yourself a used one for slaloms and save yourself a lot of grief.

Economy cars are a horse of another power. They never were intended to handle well. Some of them can be almost treacherous (see Ralph Nader).

There are many, many things that can be done to improve their handling. You can start at the back bumper and work toward the front, one piece at a time. But be careful if you intend to stay in a "stock" class. Your competitors can become quite upset if they suspect that your little innocent buggy has changed its stripes.

Catalogs are full of handling items for VW, Renaults, and cars of that ilk. Send for a "wish book" and spend as much as your budget allows. Remember, concentrate more on handling than the engine compartment. That additional 10 hp. you might buy will only gain you a couple of feet on a slalom straightaway. You can make up more than that by going through that far turn at 10 mph. faster.

Most economy imports have rear engines. Rear engines invariably couse oversteer. To reduce oversteer to controllable limits, positive camber must be run on the front and negative camber on the rear. Presumably by now, you experienced VW slalomists are rolling on the floor laughing.

Books have been written on how to make these cars handle. Buy one. A career can be spent learning to set up a rear-engined car for slaloms. Let's keep it simple. To be competitive, you will at least need: wider wheels, a camber compensator, heavier shocks, quick steering adaptor, smaller steering wheel, faster shifter, and an extractor exhaust. Whew!

You can probably get the whole works for an additional $300 – $400, depending on what kind of wheels you like. Take it for what it's worth: these cars are a heck of a lot of fun to drive, and the more enthusiastic you become, the more specialized equipment you're going to want.

At your next slalom, wander over to the class champion who drives the same kind of car you do and tell him that you sure wish that you could drive as well as he can. He will most likely almost fall backward off the stack of tires he's sitting on in his haste to explain just why his car handles so well. Listen!

Small Sports Cars

The term "small" can be misleading in this case. Small often implies *slow*. But here it doesn't. Slaloms are duck soup for a light, nimble, fast-turning sportscar. Lotuses, Sprites, and Midgets have taken many a "Fast Time of Day" trophy away from supposedly faster cars.

I can't think of a prettier sight than a bright red Lotus Elan dancing through the pylons under the hands of an experienced driver.

The winning edge in these classes is preparation and technique. Technique will be covered later in the book.

Competition in these classes is stiff, because the cars are so similar. I've often suspected that a friend of mine has never won in his Sprite because he's fifty pounds too fat!

Horsepower is very difficult to increase. The engines already are tuned close to the ultimate. Changing

Austin-Healey's can be converted to 289-302 CID Ford engines. They give close-to-Cobra performance at a fraction of a Cobra's cost.

spark plugs before every slalom is just taken for granted. You will need every edge you can get. Changing one or two pounds of air in the tires could knock .001 minute off your time.

Preparation being as important as it is, means that you'll spend every Saturday before a slalom tuning, adjusting, and polishing. Amazing how a clean car goes faster than a dirty one!

Parts that show wear must be replaced. You can't skimp on brake pads and shock absorbers and hope to win in this class.

You can spend as much money as you like. Completely blueprinted engines and competition suspensions are common at the bigger slaloms. The little guy will soon find out that the degree of preparation has a great deal to do with the placement of the car in the final standings.

Many of the winning cars will be stripped down ex-race cars that a street machine couldn't touch. This is where the "stock" classes can save your neck. Most clubs have refined the stock rules to the point that only

Even older Corvettes, because of their smaller size and lighter weight, can be *very* competitive.

Formula cars are becoming increasingly common at slaloms—a real threat for FTD.

a street, factory-stock vehicle can qualify.

The competition in the stock classes is fierce, but it's the best place to find out if you can cut the mustard.

Large Sports Cars

Large sportscars are the cars that cause a hush to fall over the crowd as they rumble and snort up to the line. They probably are the most difficult cars to master. Horsepower can be as much of a handicap as an asset. Witness the L-88 Corvette traveling sideways down the course in a cloud of tire smoke.

It takes discipline to keep your foot from stomping the loud-pedal. If you drive one of these cars, you will have to learn that tire-smoking and fishtailing may look fast to your girlfriend, but they are most assuredly *not* the way to win at slaloming.

Since Corvettes, Cobras and related vehicles already have as much horsepower as they need, we'll talk more about adapting them to typical tight slalom courses.

Many of the suspension set-up tricks for pony cars also apply here. But to a lesser degree, because these cars have much better basic suspension systems.

Factory H.D. suspensions are very good, generally having been racing tested. They are expensive to improve upon. Since this writer's experience has been mainly in Corvettes, (having owned eight of them), most of this section will be devoted to these fine cars. Slalomists no longer doubt that the Corvette is a sports car. In the midwest, Corvettes have probably taken more fast-time-of-day trophies than any other single kind of car.

A 1971 LT-1 probably has the greatest handling potential of any factory mass-produced car. The small block engine is virtually unbeatable on a tight course. Nobody seems to have come up with a really good reason why a 435 hp 'Vette with H.D. suspension, or an L-88, is not better than say a 350 hp, 350 cu. in. car. Some people say there simply is too much horsepower, others say that the most experienced drivers just happen to have small blocks. Whatever the reason, not many enthusiasts will deny that a 427/454 has its work cut out for it.

This writer's best slalom car was a 1969 Corvette 350 hp., with 3.55 rear, wide-ratio four-speed and headers. It was never beaten by a large-block Corvetta, Cobra, or whatever.

The problem in all large-engined light cars is traction. Corvette/Cobras are no exception. Tires are the greatest single asset. It is an absolute necessity that you get the proper tires, whether street or race tires. For the street class, nothing but 60 series are acceptable. B.F. Goodrich TA's are superb. Stay away from the old style narrow radials. They can not handle the torque of cornering side-thrust. Their rubber is too hard, and they're too slippery.

Race tires are a book by themselves. Compounds and sizes change yearly, and what is the ultimate this year will be outdated next year.

On a Corvette, you're going to want race tires with a 24 to 25 inch diameter and a 9 to 10 inch tread width. The current hot tire is a 10.55 × 15 by Goodyear. It uses a soft compound, and the size just clears the rear suspension control arm (after the emergency brake cable is removed or clamped down with a hose clamp).

The only way to go is to mount your race tires on a spare set of 15″ × 8″ rims and carry them to the event in a trailer or a station wagon.

The degree you go to in setting up your car depends on how much street use you require. Suspension can be reworked to the point of making street use impossible or, at the least, very, very uncomfortable.

Complete suspension systems, either installed or in kit form, can be purchased from Dick Guldstrand of Culver City, California. The advice he'll give you is slalom-tested and excellent.

The front alignment settings for the Camaro will be very effective on Corvettes and similar cars. That is, approximately 3° pos. caster and 3° neg. camber. On independent rear-ends, decamber to 2°-3° negative to plant your rear tires flatter in a turn.

A flatter, smaller, foam-rimmed steering wheel will take off some time for you. The small diameter, in effect, increases the steering ratio. Shifting is easy enough on a 'Vette. A Hurst shifter is fine for street and drag racing, but it is not intended for a fast shift from 3rd to 1st, or 4th to 2nd. It will occasionally jam and not go into gear on a downshift.

If you replace your shocks, stick with either the factory H.D. 427 shocks, or go with Koni. The Koni's have the advantage of actually improving the street ride over the stock H.D. shocks.

You won't need much more horsepower. Just tune your engine to give instant throttle response.

If you're going to order a new 'Vette for slaloming, go with either the 270 or 330 hp., 350 cu. in. engine. The wide-ratio 4-speed is better because of improved gear multiplication in 1st, 2nd, and 3rd. The rpm. drop going into 4th gear will mean nothing to you in normal driving. How often have you actually ever speed-shifted into 4th gear at 100 mph?

Don't order the H.D. brake package. These pads are designed to operate at extremely high temperatures, and they will never get hot enough at a slalom.

Stock machinery in a stock class has a pretty good chance of winning, simply because the other guy generally is not prepared much better than you are. Of course, if you want to stack the odds in your favor, a little preparation goes a long way.

A Healey-Ford, the "Poor Man's Cobra"

Chauncey Martin's Healey-Ford has been the terror of Wisconsin slaloms ever since the first day it rumbled out of the garage. It's not pretty, but it has a strange, almost brutal appeal about it. His car has taken more Fast-Time-of-Day trophies than he can remember.

If you have a limited budget, as most of us do, and you've always pictured yourself beating Corvettes and Cobras in a $500 car, this is just what you've been waiting for. But let Chauncey tell you, in his own words, what is basically involved in putting a 289 Ford into an Austin-Healey, and making it work.

"It all started about four years ago. My stock 1963 Austin-Healey 3000 didn't have a ghost of a chance against a Corvette. (They were both in the same class back then.) A Corvette could out-drag me on the straightaway, and out-corner me on the corners. I had owned the Healey since it was new and I liked it. But it needed more power, and more rubber on the ground. Much, much more power...

"With a couple of cooperative buddies, we jumped in with both feet. One "poor man's Cobra" coming up!

"A lot of Healey conversions use Chevy power, from 283 to 350 cubic inches, but a Ford 289 is 90 pounds lighter and smaller to boot. To get a Chevy in low enough you'll have to notch the frame to clear the starter. With a Ford positioned properly, your frame can stay intact.

"The local junk yards soon yielded a 4-barrel 289 Ford engine (225 HP) that was in almost new condition. A 302 or 351 will work just as well, if not better. We choose the 289 for its fast-winding characteristics. You don't need a whole lot of torque on a car as light as the Healey. Better stay away from the 351 Cleveland engine though... we think the heads may be a little too wide. Plenty of good engines are available for around $200. If you're lucky, you'll find a 4-speed transmission for another $150.

"The next parts to locate are exhaust manifolds (we used Ford Galaxie), motor mounts (a stock Ford item), and miscellaneous parts like radiator hoses. Remember, if you acquire any bastard parts, get the year and model they came from. It makes it a lot easier to replace them if the need ever arises.

"Now let's get our hands dirty. The easiest part of the job is pulling out the old Healey engine, transmission and overdrive. We weighed the Healey stuff we removed and the Ford parts we put in. Would you believe that the new parts were 130 pounds lighter! The English make nice heavy engines — if you ever need a boat anchor. Appreciate this: You're doubling your horsepower and removing weight at the same time.

"You'll probably lower the Ford into its new home at least a dozen times before you're ready to finally bolt it in. Don't get discouraged. We found some fatique cracking around the old engine mounts. Two angle-rods bolted in a box configuration around the frame took care of that. The engine's location is critical. It should be high enough so that the bottom of the pan is about ½ inch above the frame. Box spacers were made to raise the engine mounts to the proper height. The forward location will be determined by the driveshaft length, which remains stock. Usually the engine will end up about ½ inch ahead of the firewall.

"To accomplish this engine position, the transmission hump inside the body is going to have to be significantly altered. This is about the hardest job. It might be easier to simply fabricate a new hump to the larger dimensions and weld it in place of the old hump, previously having cut the old one out, of course. Make the new tunnel 2 inches wider on the right side, 3 inches wider on the left, and 3 inches lower.

"The rear engine/trans. mount is stock Ford. An extra U-channel support must be welded across the X portion of the frame to accomodate it. Your shift lever should end up in the same location as the original Healey.

"The drive-shaft was a pleasant surprise. The Ford and Healey U-joint bearing cups have the same width and outside diameter. You can use the stock Healey drive-shaft. The yoke on the transmission side of the shaft must be milled a little to accept the Ford internal snap-rings, but everything else remains the same.

"You can use the stock Ford exhaust manifold, but you'll have to change the angle of the bottom outlet to clear the floorboards. We welded up the old outlet, opened up a new one ahead of it and angled the pipe downward. Tubing exhaust headers would be nice to have, but they are very difficult to make. Save that project for next year.

"We have had good success using the stock Healey radiator. Turn it 180 degrees and mount it ahead of the front crossmember. Weld on some larger inlet and outlet spouts to accept the new larger Ford hoses.

"Use a regular Ford accelerator pedal and its cable linkage.

"The stock Healey clutch slave cylinder is retained. Bolt the slave unit to the right-hand side of the Ford bellhousing, the same as it was on the Healey engine. Keep the pedal cylinder and hydraulic lines in the same location.

"The alternator was turned *up* on its mountings, to get additional brake-line clearance. The electrical conversion was very easy. The only problem you may have from changing the "ground" is in the radio.

"Don't worry about the stock Healey rear-end. It's beefy enough for most drivers. However, if you want to win some slalom trophies, you'd better budget for a Detroit Locker rear-end (cost about $180). Power is useless if you can't make it stick to the ground. Don't count pennies on your rear suspension. Racing tires put a tremendous strain on the drive train. It must be beefed up to take this strain. Make up a set of traction-bars; they're very necessary. Reinforce the spring hangers and add another leaf to the spring if you can. Any good auto spring shop could give you plenty of good ideas.

"Wheel adapters are needed to fit 15" × 8" Corvette wheels to the hubs. The adapters also serve as spacers to increase inside tire clearance. They can be either purchased or fabricated.

"A set of race-tires completes your slalom needs. The best sizes range somewhere around 10.55 or 11.30. These Goodyears offer over 9 inches of rubber with only a 25 inch diameter. They'll just barely fit. Run around 22 to 24 pounds of air for best results.

"Something you might consider is adding a roll-bar and cage. The chassis will like the additional bracing and it may keep some scratches off the top of your helmet someday.

"As you gain driving experience you can start modifying the engine for more power. An easy 400 HP is available with just bolt-on parts. Last year we added high-performance big-valve heads, a hot cam and solid lifters, 12.5 to 1 pistons, a 780 Holley carb and hi-rise manifold.

"Now we've really got ourselves a package of dynamite that nearly takes your head off when you "punch it"..."

Note: Chauncey's conversion has stood up very well in combat. If you have any questions about this conversion, write Clarence Martin at 139 South 1st St., Milwaukee, Wisconsin. He can supply you with engine-mount drawings, wheel adapters, or anything else you might need.

An MGB, Properly Set Up

Dick Luening's MGB has a virtually unmatched string of victories to its credit. His class is a tough one. His method is to drive hard. The car he competes in is driven daily on the street. We'll let you in on some of Dick's secrets that separate winners from "also-rans"...

"First of all, understand that the type of course you will be running is going to have a great effect on how you set up your car. Because of the many, many factors that must be weighed and evaluated, the best we can do is set up the car for the majority of courses. Slaloms in my area are generally tight and bumpy. Most parking-lot slaloms fit this description. We'll set up on this premise.

"The first thing you are going to want to do is to visit your local MG dealer and order competition shock-absorber valves (front #C-AHH7217, rear #C-AHH7218). They cost around $10 each and are well worth it. When installing these valves, you'll have to remove the shock bodies from the car. Clean them out with #2 fuel oil before installing the new valves. The fuel oil will clean out the sediment without hurting the seals. When you reassemble them, with the new valves, fill them with 20W non-detergent oil before you put them back on the car. (If you don't drive your "B" on the street, fill them with 30W non-detergent oil). These shocks are very effective. You'll notice the difference.

"Undoubtedly you have heard that Koni shocks are wonderful. But because of the cost, and the fact that you can only get them for the rear, I would not recommend them for the MGB. In addition, they mount on a bracket on the rear leaf spring, which makes it very difficult to mount traction bars.

"Traction bars are very, very important. They not only stop wheel hop on rough surfaces, but they help keep the power going to the ground smoothly. They also help keep the rear spring from breaking. The best traction bars you can get, you can make yourself." (Dick Luening can sell you a set for $20, or send you a drawing with dimensions. Dick's address is 2460A S. 15th Place, Milwaukee, Wisconsin).

"You must have a front sway-bar. See your dealer or junk yard for new or used parts. The stock sway-bar is 9/16″ in diameter. If you can, try a MGB-GT bar which is ⅝″ in diameter and will help even more. If you really want something special, get a ¾″ diameter bar from your dealer. This special competition bar is part No. C-AHH7924.

"As far as rear sway-bars go, the only place they

will help any is on a road-course, or in a slalom in the rain. If you ever have to beat a Porsche on a wet, tight course, the rear bar may be the edge you need. J.C. Whitney sells a good rear bar for $20. (part no. 55-1439)

"For a really super slalom set-up you can go to a two-inch lowered 480 lbs. rate competition front coil-springs (#CHT-21). But these heavy springs should only be used with racing tires.

"Stock front camber on an MGB is ½ degrees negative. This can be increased to as much as 2 degrees with surprising results, but it's not recommended for street use. To obtain 2 degrees negative, sandwich a three/eights thick plate between the lower A-frame and the main cross-member. Remember though, this much camber may not be the ultimate on all types of courses.

"Your MGB should now be competitive with any car in its class. There are several things you can do to make your car easier to drive. When you can see the course better, turn the steering wheel and shift easier, you'll drive faster.

"A good trick is to stuff a blanket under the driver's seat cushion. It will prevent the cushion from squashing down and you'll be sitting higher. You can see the pylons better and you'll get increased leverage on the steering wheel.

"If you're driving an older "B" car, your seat may be tilted back too far, making it hard to reach 3rd gear. There are adjusting screws under the seat back. Adjust the seat so that when you're strapped in, 3rd gear is an easy reach.

"Competition seat-belts and shoulder harnesses are very effective in holding you upright when you're fighting the steering wheel. Speaking of the steering wheel, the MGB wheel is pretty good. But they have been known to break or splinter during a slalom. A sliver in your hand can hurt. A leather or foam replacement wheel is better, but stay with the original diameter. You need the leverage on a tight course.

"MGB wire-rims are 4½" wide, the steel wheels are 4". (Newer MGB-GT have 5" steel wheels). 165-14 radials will fit all of these rims. Inflate your radials to 35-45 PSI front and 30-40 PSI rear. On a wet surface, I run about the same pressures." (The author feels differently, but of course he does not own an MGB)

"Tire pressure is one of the most important changes you can make. Try running at different pressures. A pound or two difference may knock several .001's off your time. If your area doesn't have a rim width ruling, run Chevy II rims in place of your steel bolt-ons. If you like wires, you can get some 5½ inchers from British Leyland (#AHH-8530) or from good old J.C. Whitney (89-9537) for $42.95 each.

"For racing rubber, use 5.00/8.30-14 which will fit on your somewhat narrow wheels. Inflate them from 30 to 38 PSI. But for all-around slalom use I recommend Bridgestone radials, made in Japan. They give beautiful traction. But don't expect them to last as long as the harder European radials.

"There are several little things that can be done to your car at the event to give it more horsepower. Try disconnecting the wires that lead to the generator. This will give you 4 to 5 more horses. Next, weather permitting, the fan should be removed and the bolts replaced. Fine-tune the carburetors. To do this, re-move the air-cleaners and listen to the air-flow inside the carbs. Adjust the idle screws on the top of the carb until the air-flows sound alike. Champion N-9Y have been found to be the best spark plugs. Instead of going deeper into the engine and doing things like polishing the ports, milling the head, or grinding the combustion chambers, buy the books "Special Tuning for the MGB" and the "Work Shop Manual"

(#AKD3259F) from your dealer. But if you ever do pull the engine, have the reciprocating parts balanced.

"The standard 3.91 rear axle ratio in the "B" is adequate. But if you can afford it, get a Detroit Locker in 4.88 ratio. They cost around $180 and are worth every penny. When buying gas, I always get Sunoco 260 and try to arrive at the event with about 4 gallons in the tank.

"I sure hope that you guys appreciate the tips we're giving you. I hope that nobody from my area buys this book... because he'll know every one of my tricks and he'll be damn tough to beat."

Tires, Trailers, Tuning

After you have run a number of events, a set of race tires will look better and better. Your car will never realize its full potential on street tires. Adhesion is the weakest link. Race tires are cheaper than you might imagine. Goodyears and Firestones run about the same price, $35 to $55 each, depending on size and type. Firestone has been phasing out race tire production, so you're better off with Goodyear.

Don't attempt to run your hairy-looking racing tires on the street, because you'll have nothing but grief. The tires are so thin that if you run over a grasshopper leaping in the air, you'll get a flat tire! Race tires steer terribly at slow speed on a bumpy road. Your car will "dance" all over the road.

The latest tubeless Indy style tires will leak air through the sidewalls and will virtually go "flat" every week. Mount the tires on a separate set of rims and carry them to the slalom. Try to avoid even driving to the event on your race tires. All it takes is one blown tire to kill you for that event if you don't have a matching spare. A set of tires will last almost two full seasons, depending of course on how many Sundays you run and what kind of car you drive.

It pays to buy five tires of the same size and compound. Race tires are constantly being improved and sizes are eliminated several times a year. To be sure you have a set of tires for the season, buy that extra one tire of a size that nobody has any more.

Don't discount buying "used" racing tires. They only cost $25 each, and many of them are just like new. The best time to buy used tires is during the winter. Your racing tire distributor generally is well stocked with used tires during the off-season.

To buy the right size tire, see what your competitors are using. It doesn't make sense to first buy the tire and then try to make it fit your fenderwells afterward. Most drivers buy tires that are too big. The larger tire does not offer that much more tread. You shouldn't have to worry about tearing up your sidewalls every time you hit a bump on a slalom course.

If you are going to be very active in autocrosses, you should get yourself a second car. Any jalopy is fine. All you want is a second car in case something breaks on the sporty model. You can drive faster if you don't have to worry about breaking something and getting to work on a Monday morning.

It also pays to line up a trailer to carry your car home if you break it. Trailer rental agencies have car trailers to rent on a one day basis. Keep their phone number in your wallet, just in case. And line up a friend with a strong trailer hitch on his car. There's a good chance that there's someone in your car club that has a race car trailer. If you plan ahead, you can eliminate those worries about "breaking down" that frustrate so many slalomists.

Quite often you will hear the argument that a street-driven slalom car has no chance against an out-and-out ex-race car. Don't you believe it. A true race car is like a bull in a china shop when it comes to slaloms. Their engines are tuned to a narrow, high rpm. torque curve, say, from 5500 to 6500 rpm. Obviously, this is totally unsuited to our purposes. Usually their brakes are designed only to function at very high temperatures; temperatures that they will never attain in a slalom. Many times their suspensions are too stiff for a typical bumpy slalom course.

Our street engines are more flexible, pull from lower rpm., don't overheat in the staging line, and they "start" every time. Our street brakes give a softer pedal, work when cold, and never get hot enough to fade. Don't sell a street-machine short. It is an excellent slalom choice.

Every car, no matter what kind or type, has its absolute cornering limit, which may be faster or slower than some other car. We'll call this absolute limit for a given car "100%." That is, if a corner is attempted at 101%, the car will spin out. You want to drive your car at as close to 100% as you possibly can. If you can hold 98% or 99% on every corner on the course, no one in your type of car will ever beat you. But remember, a better set-up car than yours will be going faster when it reaches its 100%. The driver of this faster car may only have to hold 85%-90% to beat your 95%-96%, because his car can corner at 20% higher speed.

What all this is meant to show is that if you are doing a tremendous job of driving your car, even if nobody could drive it better, and some clown beats you, don't feel discouraged. Many times you will be beaten simply because the other guy has better equipment.

Even a Mario Andretti or a Jackie Stewart would lose at a slalom if he were driving the wrong equipment. We try to set up our classes based on a car's potential, but there are always a couple of cars in every class that are virtually guaranteed a trophy, even if they're only driven at 75% of potential. Just grin and bear it. Or go out and buy yourself a better car.

It takes strong discipline and self-control to drive the hotter modifieds well.
Their acceleration is brutal.

Chapter IV

THE DRIVER

This section will give you the winning pointers that have helped average drivers become winners. Try to absorb as many of the techniques as you can. Take this book along with you to slaloms as a middle-of-the-day reference guide before you take your last run.

There are several specific subjects that we will discuss:

1) Attitude
2) Natural ability
3) Awareness techniques
4) Psychological techniques or "Oneupsmanship"
5) Driving techniques
6) Strategy
7) Equipment

Attitude

You are going to have to put yourself in a positive frame of mind. Tell yourself that you are going to win. That you are now going to drive faster than you ever have before. Make beating your last run's time your sole purpose in life. Convince yourself that you can do whatever you set your mind to. Push yourself to get every last bit out of your car. Strain yourself and your machinery to the extreme limit.

These mental exercises are best performed as you are waiting in the staging line, one or two slots back from the start line. If your competition comes up to talk to you, don't encourage conversation in these last few minutes. Just nod your head. Don't break your concentration. A slalom course demands as much intense,

Owners of competition cars find slaloms a good place to get some of the bugs out of their cars before their next road race.

A row of pylons like this will separate the men from the boys. Here is where a smooth, steady driver makes up time.

instant energy as any other physical competition: swimming, pole vaulting or high jumping. You must get yourself "keyed up" before you ever leave the start line.

As you are waiting to make your run, tell yourself that this run is going to be your best yet. That you are going to correct the mistakes you made before. That you are really going to "show everybody." Keep these thoughts going through your mind until you hit the gas pedal and start your run.

Natural Ability

If you have normal reaction times, you can push yourself hard enough to win any slalom. You will simply have to try harder than the guy with quicker-than-average reflexes.

If you wear eyeglasses, get a prescription that corrects your vision to 20-10, which is better than normal. Every little edge can help you.

Even your physical condition is important. Slaloms are a physical sport, and you should be in shape. A couple of months before the season starts, get in the habit of doing pushups in the morning. Lose some weight if you can. Your arms and chest must be strong, especially if you drive a larger, heavier car with race tires.

Awareness Tricks

Some of these may sound strange, but they work. One of the biggest problems you may have is the tendency for your mind to wander from the job at hand. Your concentration fades as you're driving through the course. Maybe your thoughts dwell on that last gate you took or whether your girlfriend is watching.

You must keep your mind out in **front** of your car.

To increase your awareness while you're driving, TALK to yourself out loud. Urge yourself to go faster. Talk to your car. Talk to the pylons. It seems foolish, but it keeps your mind doing the proper things.

Another gimmick is to chew gum. The gum serves

Put yourself in the right frame of mind *before* you leave the starting gate. Half way around the course is too late.

Before you get to the start line, put your helmet and gloves on. Check your seatbelt, and warm up your engine.

A timid driver will never do well at a slalom. The trick is to be aggressive, yet smooth.

as an outlet for your anger when you knock over that damn pylon. Yes, you can talk to yourself and still chew gum at the same time.

Fasten your seat belt and helmet strap uncomfortably tight. The pain also helps to keep you aware of your surroundings.

Psychological Tricks

A good way to beat your competition is to "psych" them out. Usually there's only one guy that you have to beat. If he's a buddy of yours, it's easier. Here are some of the things you can tell him:

A)"Say, Ralph, your engine sounds pretty bad... sort of like a connecting rod is pounding. Could you hear it out on the course?"

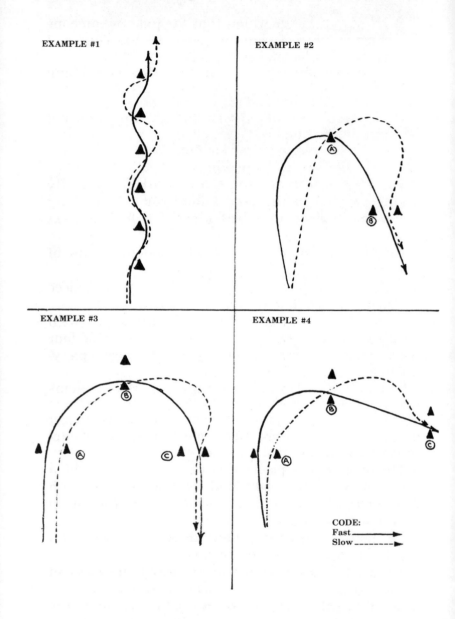

EXAMPLE #1

EXAMPLE #2

EXAMPLE #3

EXAMPLE #4

CODE:
Fast ───────▶
Slow ─ ─ ─ ─ ▶

These are the four examples of driving techniques referred to in the text.

B) "Boy, you better watch that far pylon - someone must have lost some oil all over the course. I pretty near lost it."

C) "Did you know that your front tire is rubbing when you turn the wheel sharp? It was really smoking on your last run."

D) "I'm going to take it easy today - the car's not running so hot."

All's fair in love, war, and slaloms...

Techniques

The idea is to make the course work for you. By taking a pylon in the proper line, you'll be moving faster and end up in a better position for the next gate.

Keep your mind at least several pylons ahead of the car.

Walk around the course; study it. Draw it on a piece of paper and sketch in the quickest route.

Using the "driving techniques" drawings, we'll go through the slow and fast lines for each of four basic types of pylon sequences. See the accompanying drawings.

Example #1: A typical row of pylons. Most slaloms include these somewhere on the course. They are one of your most basic problems. Once you learn to get through these properly, the same principles will apply to many different situations.

The idea in this problem is to go in as straight a line as possible. To turn the steering wheel in smooth equal amounts from left to right, maintaining a steady throttle. You want your car to virtually dance in a perfectly synchronized pattern. A beautiful sight to see when properly done.

The inexperienced driver will find that he will end up out of phase with the pylons, and he'll often knock down the last one. Each mistake he makes is compounded at the next pylon. Soon his course is farther and farther away from each pylon, and it's harder and harder to turn sharply enough to avoid hitting the next one.

Remember, smoothness is the most important aspect. Don't try to brake or accelerate halfway through the series. Learn your maximum cornering speed through experience, and hold this speed as you maneuver through.

A much more tricky technique you'll find at some events is to stagger the spacing between pylons in a row. This won't allow you to get a smooth left and right swing going and makes it much more difficult. You will have to study this staggered pattern carefully and lay out your route.

Example #2: Most drivers invariably head directly for pylon (A). By doing so, the farthest point of their turn is far beyond the desired location, which makes them double-turn to get back to where they should have been.

The idea is to start your turn far to the left and well before you reach pylon (A). Since turning radii and turning speeds are always the same in your car, you want to make them work for you by placing your turning "pattern" in exactly the right spot. By appreciating your turning radius, you can easily knock 30-40 feet off the distance you travel in negotiating example #2.

Example #3: This geometric pylon pattern is the ideal example of what should be a fast, smooth constant radius 180° turn. Our inexperienced friend will generally convert this into two or three corners with great sliding and fishtailing.

The way to take this corner is to edge over to the left pylon at (A), just nick the inside pylon at (B), and slide out to nick the outside pylon at (C). You should balance your car with steering and throttle around the loop, keeping it in a four wheel drift just at the edge of adhesion.

In a constant turn like this, you must be constantly making little gentle nudges on the steering wheel in kind of a sawing motion to test your cornering limit. The steering will feel very light and a little gas will cause the rear end to come around steeper. Yet it is this balance between understeer and oversteer that gives you a beautiful four wheel drift.

Example #4: This can be a very tricky corner. Many drivers will attempt to stay on the righthand side of (A) and (B), completing most of their direction change between (B) and (C).

The fast line is to complete your direction change and be pointed in the right direction before you arrive at (B). Then you can accelerate as you pass (B) and blast straight through (C).

This is another example of taking what seems to be the longer route at the beginning. Remember to keep your mind at least 2 pylons ahead of your car.

These four examples are only a few of the many patterns you will encounter. But you will find that after analyzing these problems, you will realize a new awareness at your next event.

Learn to analyze the course exactly the way you did the examples. Take along a pad of paper and draw the course. Trace the fastest route and then follow it.

One of the basic principles is to remember to take it easy on the gas pedal. Even if your car doesn't have a lot of power, you still lose time fishtailing if you try to accelerate too soon.

Remember to complete all of your braking *before* you enter a turn. When you try to turn with brakes applied, your front tires will just slide.

If there are any pylons that you must cut extremely close, disengage the clutch as you pass. With the car simply rolling free, you will often harmlessly roll over the base of the pylon without knocking it over.

As you are driving through a series of tight turns, remember to turn the wheel ahead of time to allow for your slide. Your car will always skid a few feet before it begins to turn. By anticipating this little

Corner gently, keeping your speed below the breakaway limit of the front tires.

slide, you can easily wind your way through any complicated series.

If you must make a very sharp, full steering lock turn, keep your car under the speed at which the front tires begin to plow. Don't try to accelerate or to power the tail around in an arc. It may seem fast to power the tail around, but it throws your car out of shape for acceleration. A fast technique in a really tight corner is to simply disengage the clutch and *roll* around the turn. Sounds slow, but you'd be amazed how fast your car can turn tight when it's free-rolling.

As discussed before, you must keep your mind ahead of your car. Never let your thoughts dwell on pylons you've just passed.

Notice the type of surface on the parking lot. Stay away from areas with loose sand or gravel. Your path may have to be a bit longer by avoiding these areas, but you can more than make up the time lost.

To give a little better traction, run with about ¾ of a tank of gas. The extra weight is in exactly the right spot. It's not a good idea to run with a full tank, because you may be spilling gas on the course and all over your bright, shiny fender.

On any type of course, you want to turn the steering wheel as little as possible. Try to straighten out the course as much as you can. Remember, you can neither brake nor accelerate effectively if your front wheels are not straight.

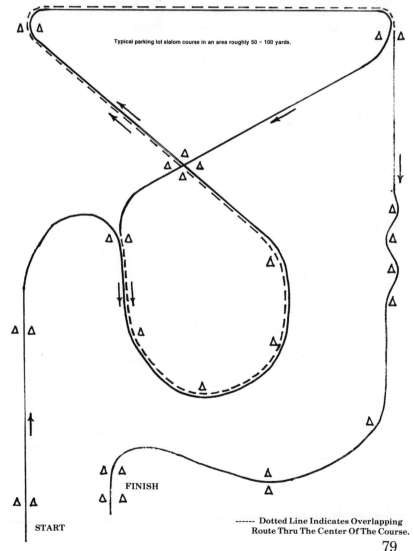

Typical parking lot slalom course in an area roughly 50 × 100 yards.

FINISH

START

------ Dotted Line Indicates Overlapping
Route Thru The Center Of The Course.

79

When you leave the start line, accelerate smoothly. Don't just dump the clutch and tromp on the gas
pedal at the same time.

Some Sunday afternoon, go to a drag strip and
watch the driving techniques of the competitors.
Notice that, by starting gently for the first few feet,
a smart driver can pick up several car lengths over
the hot-shot that smokes out of the "hole." The same
principle applies at slaloms. Your car will travel farther, faster, if you don't smoke the tires.

Strategy

By using your head, there are several things you
can do that might help you win.

Get to the event very early. Try to get as much
practice as possible-if the club allows it.

Walk completely around the course. See it from
all the different directions that you'll see it when
you're driving.

Most clubs will at least allow you to walk through
the course if you can't practice with your car.

Be able to drive through the course in your mind
before you attempt to drive it in your car. You must
know the route without thinking about it when
you're driving. There is no time for route decisions
during a fast run.

Many drivers find that runs early in the morning
are faster than in the afternoon. Tire rubber and sand
often slow the course down later in the day, and it's
cooler in the morning.

If your club does not take their runs by class - if
you can take a run whenever you want to - try to do
your thing when the staging line is the shortest.
Ideally, you might even wait to the extreme end of
the day and take your two last runs consecutively.
You want to get another run as soon as possible
after you finish one. Your mind is more alert, your
adrenalin is pumping, the course is fresh in your
mind, and your tires are still hot. Under these conditions, you are at your best.

Always wait till your competition has taken their runs before you take yours. See what their times were. This tells you how fast you are going to have to drive. Save at least one run till the very end.

Driving In The Wet

Slaloms in the "wet" are a heck of a lot of fun. Rain completely changes the odds. Horsepower is a handicap. Cars that may never have won before are suddenly competitive. Conservative, smooth, but maybe slightly slower drivers often excel on a slippery course. The aggressive technique that can win on a dry course will spin you out on a wet one.

Let's differentiate between a wet course and a damp course. Truly "wet" means puddles and pools of standing water. The kind that causes tires to hydroplane. Many times a sporadic light drizzle, or even rain, may make the course look wet, when actually it's not bad at all — just damp. An asphalt surface is usually very rough and porous. The roughness keeps things sticky.

If it is really wet, start by lowering your tire pressures 6 to 8 pounds all around. Contrary to what many drivers have been taught, less pressure will work better in a low speed slalom. Normally you would want to raise pressures when speeds are high to decrease the hydroplaning tendency. The higher pressure reduces the tire's footprint size which reduces the size and potential "lift" of the water cushion under the tire. Most parking-lot slaloms seldom exceed 60 mph., and when it's wet you won't be able to get enough traction to reach the higher speeds anyway. This writer has run as low as 15 pounds in all four tires of his Corvette, and won...

If you have radial tires, you may now grin from ear to ear. They are the best you can get for puddle splashing. If your tread is still reasonably deep you can be confident that your equipment is capable of doing the job, if you do your part. You can still run the normal 24 to 26 pounds of air. The soft sidewalls and rigid tread can really get the job done.

What you're really going to need when it's raining is "discipline". Keep the old foot off the loud pedal. Nothing will kill your chances faster than a heavy foot. It's a powerful temptation to show everybody how you're not afraid to go fishtailing around the course going backwards as often as forwards. You must control that urge. Gently apply gas as you come off a corner. Wait till the car is lined up perfectly straight. Try to sense whether the rear tires are grabbing. Wait for the traction to catch up to the engine. If you would normally come off a corner in first gear, come off in second. The reduced torque is just what the doctor ordered. Remember, horsepower is a curse in a puddle of water.

Another trick that pays off is to fill your gas tank. That extra 75 pounds or so will help over the back wheels.

Your steering control is going to be drastically reduced. Everything will seem to happen in slow motion. Knowing that you're going to slide, anticipate it. Turn the steering wheel as much as 10 feet before you get to the pylon. If your timing is just right, your slide will end up in exactly the spot you want to be.

Braking won't be as hard as you might think. You can stop much faster than you can accelerate because all four tires are working for you. Don't lock up your wheels. A gentle off-and-on pulsation on the brake pedal will stop you faster and straighter.

There are always those drivers who will try to use their emergency braks to lock up their rear wheels on a tight 180 degree corner. Their idea is to throw the car into a controlled skid which will happily end them up facing back in the direction they want to go. What they never realize is that their car will usually come to a complete stop in the process, and they will have to accelerate from a standing start. Not easy in the wet. You can try it, but don't expect to get it just right more than one out of three attempts. Remember, you might blow two of your runs experimenting.

An autocross in the rain is a memorable experience that you'll enjoy if you recognize your vehicle's limitations.

A wet course is excellent training for both dry and wet street driving. Every move you make is magnified. It takes discipline and self-control to drive fast. The rain can tell you if you have these qualities.

If it looks like rain, get your runs in as soon as possible. Don't take a chance of being caught on a wet course. It slows you down too much. You'll never equal your competitor's times if he has had a dry run.

You might even tell the event chairman that you have to leave early and ask if you could take your runs right away, consecutively. This will only work a couple of times before people begin to catch on, especially if you never leave during the day.

Equipment

Start out by making up a slalom kit to carry in the trunk of your car all the time. Then you'll never forget it. The items you'll need are:

tire gauge	pencil and pad
helmet	aspirins
driving gloves	first aid kit
sunglasses	suntan lotion
masking tape	electrical tape
shoe polish	a few simple tools

Put all this stuff in a bowling ball bag, and you're all set.

When you buy yourself a pair of driving gloves, don't get the very thin, delicate leathers. Get something more in the line of a leather dress glove, unlined. Something that is sewn from a much heavier material. They will protect your fingers much better and you'll feel more confident not having to worry about banging your fingers in the spokes.

If your steering wheel has sharp spokes, either file them smoother or wrap them in vinyl tape. You can't be worrying about hurting your hands.

Changing tires is the loneliest job in the world.

Sew one of those leather covers on your steering wheel. For a neater job, go to a hobby shop and get some regular leather lacing and a sewing needle. It makes a much more professional-looking job than the shoe laces that come with the steering wheel cover.

Presumably, you're going to wear something in a sneaker-type shoe. Get something with a sponge rubber type of sole. The artificial rubber tennis shoes that are being sold are too slippery. Another trick that works quite well is to wrap rubber electrical tape around the smooth rubber pads on your clutch and brake pedals. It just might prevent your foot from slipping off at the wrong time. If you have a foreign car with metal pedals, glue a piece of emery cloth on each pedal to really make your feet stick. The same technique will work on the rubber pedals that most of us have.

Take off your inside rear view mirror if it obscures any part of the course. You can put it back on for the drive home.

Remove every loose item from the inside of the car. You can't have anything rolling out from under your seat at a crucial time.

Take out the floor mats on both sides. You want to eliminate anything that might distract you.

If the passenger seat back does not have a catch to hold it back, tie it back with a piece of rope.

Secure or remove the spare tire and jack in your trunk. Remove everything else.

To be able to drive quickly, your car is going to have to be in tip-top shape. You can't have any worries on your mind about the left front tire being bald. Or be concerned about that loose ball-joint. Or worry that your tail pipe is going to fall off. If you keep your car in good condition, a slalom is seldom demanding enough to break anything. We have gone for years in Milwaukee without any kind of a breakdown at our events. Slaloms do strain your vehicle, but it's mainly tires and suspension that get the toughest wear. Because most runs are under one minute, you may only get three or four minutes actual driving time during the entire day. Any car in good condition can endure that.

Slaloms are the best possible way to really learn to drive. Highways are no place to practice high speed cornering techniques — not if you expect to stay alive, that is. It could justifiably be said that a good slalom driver is a far, far better driver than the average street driver. What typical "drive-to-work-every-day-in-bumper-to-bumper-traffic" driver ever has the opportunity to learn how to brake, to maneuver, to corner his car safely at a good speed? Slaloms will build your confidence in your ability to handle your car in extreme conditions. You will learn that evasion is better than braking in most traffic emergencies. You will be aware of the speeds at which your car can safely maneuver.

A good slalom driver knows that he is a good driver, and he feels no need to prove it on the highway.

Imagine yourself driving home on the expressway at

65 mph. in heavy traffic. You're maybe 60-70 feet behind the car ahead of you, a reasonable distance, in the righthand lane. You're making good time, and the traffic is moving steadily. Suddenly a rear tire blows on the station wagon ahead of you. He fishtails back and forth twice and then starts to go into a long broadslide. You realize that to brake would be foolish. Even if you could stop in time, the car behind you would probably plow into the back of your car. But knowing your car's capabilities, you simply flick the steering wheel to the right, swerving smoothly onto the shoulder of the highway without even changing speed, and you safely pass the now almost motionless disabled vehicle. You see in your rear view mirror that the car behind you has hit the station wagon broadside. You might have been smashed between those two cars. Now that you're in the clear, you can safely come to a stop and go back to help the accident victims.

You can see from our little tale that the techniques you learn on a slalom course can stay with you for the rest of your life, making you a much better driver. They could even *save* your life. Think about it.

Chapter V

"A TYPICAL SUNDAY AT A SLALOM..."

You wake up at 8:00 a.m. because you want to wash the car before you leave. It should have been washed last night, but by the time you finished changing plugs, painting the tires, and cleaning the engine, it was after dark. Feels sort of foolish washing the car at this time in the morning. But to hell with what the neighbors think - they wouldn't appreciate a good car if they saw one anyway.

Better get the Windex and clean the inside of that windshield. Open the hood and check the oil and give the chrome stuff one last wipe. Might as well take off the hub caps and trim rings now and save some time after you get there. Check to make sure that you have your "slalom kit." Sure makes it simpler when all the stuff you need is in one bag. You won't need any lunch 'cause there's a drive-in just a block away from the course.

Put the top down for the drive over. You can hear the exhaust better, and the breeze helps wake you up. You're not taking your girlfriend today, because not many of us are really lucky enough to get a woman who's willing to get up this early to go to a slalom. When you do take one along, she always seems to want to leave early, or has to go to the bathroom three times a day when the nearest restroom is five miles away. And she's always hungry, thirsty, or has a headache. If you're trying to win, it's easier by yourself. Plenty of your buddies will be there. You can make it up to your girlfriend tonight.

The drive to the event is always wonderful. The car runs great with its new plugs, and it seems to sense that it's going to race today. The mufflers sound meaner, and at idle, the whole car seems to throb. She pulls clean and pure all the way to 6500.

The roads are virtually deserted at 9:00 a.m. on Sunday morning, so you drive a little faster than you should, running it way up on the tach so you can hear that heavenly sound when you "back off." You downshift several times at each stop light. You really feel great today; the car has never run better. It's sunny, about 65 degrees, and there's only a 10% chance of showers in the late afternoon.

Keep your eyes peeled for radar traps. You never know about a Sunday morning in some of these small towns.

You're wondering how many cars there will be in your class and if Chauncey got his Healey/Ford fixed in time to run today. He's always damn tough to beat, but at least the rough competition keeps you on your toes.

Halfway there, you stop at a gas station to fill your tank up to the ¾ mark and to add some air to your tires... Think I'll try 36 front and 32 rear - I can always reduce them later if the course is bumpy.

The gas station attendant asks you if you race the car. You reluctantly nod your head affirmatively. He wouldn't know the difference between real road racing and a slalom anyway. What the hell, give the kid something to tell his friends.

Later, as you pull around the last corner just before the slalom site, you give it one final throttle blip and throw a 5000 rpm. downshift into first gear to let them know you're coming. Let 'em worry a little.

There's a pretty good crowd already. Must be 30 cars. We should get 85 today, easy.

You're glad you don't have to work at the event for a change. It'll be nice not to have to think about anything except driving. You can always give them a hand at tech or crowd control.

Park the car next to your buddies and look around to see where everyone is. They're all over at registration.

Strolling over, you try not to grin as your friends see you coming. The whole gang's here. Gary's got a new set of race tires, Rick repainted his car, and Chauncey put a new cam in his potent Healey/Ford.

You're glad you're not running race tires today, because it's going to be a rough class. Besides, changing tires is the loneliest, dullest job in the world.

Registration is well organized. You're surprised at how quickly you're walking back toward your car with your general instruction sheet, car number, flyer for the next event, and $4.00 poorer.

It's nice to have your own shoe polish. Sometimes they want to put the number on for you at tech. But today you can do it yourself. There won't be any official tech inspection, to save time. But you're subject to being inspected at any time during the day. No sweat - your car can pass any tech.

By the time you get your car numbered, cars are starting to line up. The course is still closed.

There won't be any practice, so you'd better check the course drawing on the timing van and start walking. Make a little sketch of the course on a scrap of paper and stuff it in your pocket.

With a couple of your friends, you walk through the course. Seems real simple. That far corner is going to be tight; better take the entrance wide to give yourself enough room. The rest of the course is obvious.

As you get back to your car, the first guy in line burns off the start line. He gets halfway through the course and gets lost. Whoever it was, he has an embarrassed grin on his face as he slowly drives back to the end of the staging line. A friend of his yells something to him, but you can't hear what it was.

It's nice to get an early run, but you can't afford to

get lost. If you go wrong the first run, your mind almost gets programmed to going the wrong way. You must drive the right course the first time, even if slowly.

Before you take a run, watch a couple of cars go through. Walk around the course to get views from different directions. See where the other guys are going wrong, and right.

There are about 15 cars in line already. They're not running by class, so you can take a run whenever you want to. Think you'd better get in line. The course can still be seen from the staging line. The twenty minutes you'll spend waiting can be spent studying the course.

You're staged in back of a Formula Ford. Sweet piece of equipment. Those formula cars are going to be a real threat for FTD. The Ford has to be pushed down the staging line. You give him a hand. He helps you push your car.

As you get three or four cars away from the start line, you know the course and can run it through in your head with your eyes closed. You're ready. You start your engine five minutes before you run to get it warmed up. When there are only two cars in front of you, you put on your helmet, fasten your seat belt, slip your driving gloves on, and check to make sure all the doors are securely closed.

You decide that your first run will be easy and smooth. No pushing. Just play it cool and learn the course. Let the other guys think that they'll beat you.

Sooner than you would have liked, you're next. You watch the timing light. When it turns red, you ease out the clutch and leave the line with a slight "chirp."

The pylons seem to be in exactly the right spots, because you know the course. By thinking ahead, you can anticipate the next corner, and it comes smoothly. There are no surprises.

You come off the course feeling good. It was not too fast, but you did everything right, and you're confident. No point in taking another run right away.

After the car is parked, you wander over to the timer to see what you did. You had a 1.015. That's the fastest time so far, but only fifteen cars have run, and none were the real "hot dogs." It's going to take about a .950 to win your class, you figure. You can do it.

The day goes by swiftly, what with talking to your friends, looking at cars, watching the course, and helping with staging and crowd control.

You've got two runs in, out of three possible for the day. The best time you have is .980. Rick has a .979 and lets you know it, good naturedly, about every five minutes. He has two runs also. Nobody else is close enough to worry about. They're all over 1.000 minute. A lot of drivers have three runs in already.

The race tire class times are running around .910 with Chauncey's Healey/Ford the fastest at .902. On his second run his fuel pump gave out, but he fixed it, and he's all set for his third run. He'll wait till the very end. So will we.

There's a hot competition going between the MGB's, with first place changing hands after every run. Be interesting to see who wins.

On his third run, a Saab sedan loses his front wheel in the far corner of the course. The center section broke out, and the rim came off. The fender was bent a bit, but the spindles and tie rods were O.K. His wheel was replaced with his spare, and he drove off the course, all in only ten minutes. But his wife wasn't too happy!

The sky is getting very dark, and guys are joking about feeling raindrops. There are only ten or so cars that haven't had their third run yet. You wait...

Finally Rick breaks down and goes to get his car. After an endless fifteen minute wait in line, he finally takes his run. It's flawless. You wonder if you could ever look that good or even hope to beat him. His run is smooth, he follows a precise course, and he never touches a pylon. You can hear the spectators mumbling compliments and praise for the impressive drive. The timer posts a time of .969, the fastest street tire time of the day. Your heart sinks. You're really going to have to push to beat that, if you can. You congratulate Rick on a tremendous run, and you mean it.

There are only three cars left in line when you pull up behind them. They had the same idea you did. Chauncey rolls his Healey/Ford up behind you. He's the last car to run.

Now you're only two cars away from the start line. Your helmet, seat belt, and gloves are on. Your engine sounds right on, at 180°. The entire day flashes before your eyes. You run through the course in your mind over and over. The car is perfect; *it* can do it. Can you?

You tell yourself that you are going to drive faster than you ever have before. You are going to push your Corvette to the absolute limit. You know you can do it...

Drops of rain begin to spatter your windshield. People run for their cars.

Why, why, did it have to rain? You're the next car out. But the parking lot is porous, and it takes several minutes to get really wet. This is your only hope.

You switch on your wipers. Damn rain! The light goes red. Your mind goes blank, and all you can see is the course ahead of you. As you leave the line, you notice that your tires are grabbing just as well as before, and you know that you made it just in time. Two or three minutes more, and the course would have been too wet.

You talk to yourself as you wind your way through the pylons, saying things like, "Attaboy", "Faster, faster", "Watch that next gate", "Hit it, hit it", "Easy"...

As you blast toward the finish line, you are completely exhausted. You wonder if you'll be able to turn the wheel for that last gate. With your last strength, you barely manage to make the last gate, just nicking the outside pylon. You don't know how you did. Did the rain slow you down? Was it as fast as your last run?

You roll down the pit line, unfastening your helmet and seat belt, and swing into a parking slot.

As you open the door, two of your buddies come running over with big smiles on their faces. One of them is Rick. Oh god, you think, he must have beaten me...

".965," he yells, ".965." "You bastard," Rick laughs, shaking my hand and thumping me on the back, with rain running down our faces.

Everything else is anticlimactic. I drive home slowly, with the wipers on and the radials hissing on the road, with the trophy lying on the seat beside me, still wet.

I don't care if the other cars on the road pass me. I'm completely at peace with the world and don't have to prove a thing to anybody.

"I won this time, but can I do it the next?"...

The author in a typical position.

Chapter VI

TRI-STATE
SPORTSCAR CONFERENCE
1971 SLALOM RULES

The *Tri-State Sportscar Conference* is an example of what can be done by a dedicated group of slalomists. Their organization, started in 1964, was formed to encourage honest competition thru standardized classes and rules in a three state area.

The idea has proven to be very successful. At present the following Clubs are affiliated with this fine group:

> Austin-Healey Club
> American Motors Car Club, Chicago
> American Motors Car Club, Milwaukee
> Chicagoland Corvair Enthusiasts
> Concours Plaines Rallye Team
> Lake Region Sportscar Club
> Lotus Corps
> Mid-West Sportscar Club
> Milwaukee Sportscar Club
> Mustang Club of Chicago
> Northern Illinois Sportscar Club
> SCCA, Chicago Region
> Sportscar Club of Chicago

The *Tri-State* rules and classes are reproduced in the following chapter for your use as a guide in your area. These rules have evolved over a seven year period and have survived countless protests.

Section

> A   Gym-Div & Club Administration of Series
> B   Slalom Course Design

C   Event Administration
D   Timing & Scoring Procedures
E   Scoring System for the Championship Series
F   Competitor Procedures and Eligibility
G   Car Preparation & Eligibility
H   Class Definitions
I   Protest Procedures
    Car Classes

Gym-Div Championship Slalom Series
1971 General Rules

Foreword - The following are the regulations governing the Championship Slaloms sanctioned by the Tri-State Sportscar Conference (TSSCC). The conference, thru the Gym-Div, forms these regulations in order that Championship Slaloms can be conducted on an equitable basis for all entrants.

Section A Gym-Div & Club Administration of Series

A1   Championship programs will be *only* straight forward driving competitions on paved surfaces, without oncourse stops or backups (gymkhanas, slaloms, and autocrosses). No passengers or navigators are allowed.

A2   Luck or chance may not be deliberately included as a factor in judging.

A3   All championship programs (shown as *Ch. Slalom* thruout this code) must be previewed and approved at a closed meeting, at least two weeks before the event date. The sanctioning committee of three will include the Chief Steward and/or the Championship Coordinator, and the balance to be made up of the Gym-Div board members.

A4   At the preview, the sponsoring club must furnish proof of insurance covering their proposed program, as well as organizational details and all other materials prepared for their program. (Flyer, Registration, Tech, Course layout, Timing, Scoring, Trophy awards system, Safety, and other related paperwork. Only TSSCC Tech and Registration forms will be used.)

A5 Competitors & Sponsors of Gym-Div sanctioned programs *must* agree in writing to abide by the General Rules in force at that time. Failure to abide, on the part of either party, leaves them liable to official protest to Gym-Div. (See Sect. 1)

A6 Any additional rules of the sponsoring club may not conflict with any part of this code; must apply uniformly to all entrants; is necessary for safety or the conduct of the program; & must be approved by the preview committee.

A7 A copy of this code *must* be displayed at every *Ch. Slalom* registration area.

A8 The Gym-Div board has the authority to override any sponsoring club's interpretation of this code.

A9 All questions on this code, or car performance options, must be submitted in writing to the Steward's committee. A written reply will be made.

A10 This code may be revised by a two-thirds majority of Gym-Div representatives of member clubs present and voting at a regularly announced meeting. Rule changes will take effect *only* after 15 days following a mailing of the change to all registered drivers.

Section B Slalom Course Design

B1 Events at a *Ch. Slalom* will be staged only on surfaces approved by the preview committee (with a final OK on site before the start of competition). The course area must be free from unsafe holes, loose areas, gratings, and other unsafe situations.

B2 Courses will be roped off or otherwise isolated, with spectators kept a safe distance from the course. A 50 ft. minimum distance (from centerline of course lane) is required if steel or concrete dividers are not present.

B3 Course layout must be the same for all entrants, & not changed in any way after competition has begun, unless safety dictates. Once changed, all cars will run the revised course.

B4 The location of all course markers must be marked so that they can be returned to their original position if displaced. Marker location should be checked at regular intervals during the course of the program.

B5 Displaced markers will be replaced before the next competitor starts his timed run or he shall be granted a rerun.

B6 Where an official run covers all or part of the course twice, course marshals should have extra markers available to replace those moved before the competing car returns to that section of the course.

B7 Courses must be laid out so that all normally accepted cars can negotiate the courses without reversing. All gates will be a minimum of 12 ft. wide, measured from the insides of markers; markers in a series (as a slalom) should be at least 30 ft. apart.

B8 All course markers must be such that they are easily visible, as approved by the Gym-Div preview committee.

B9 The maximum length of any one straightaway, measured from turn to turn, will be 100 yds. A turn is defined as a change of direction of at least 30°. This rule may be waived by the preview committee, for the use of natural road courses.

B10 Course layout will be posted or mapped in a clear way, for all entrants to see before timed runs start.

B11 No start/finish may be used where driver is not in vehicle with seatbelt buckled and helmet on head.

B12 There should be a minimum of one (1) minute judged time. Judged time is the average elapsed time on course, per run, by which the program is scored.

Section C Event Administration

C1 All championship drivers should receive notice of a *Ch. Slalom* at least *two weeks* prior to the program date. Include information on Date, Sponsoring club, Event name, Location, Registration, Starting time, Price, Tech, and Preregistration instructions if applicable.

C2 If the sponsoring club feels it is necessary to conduct practice or familiarization runs, then equal opportunity for the runs must be given to all entrants. Time for practice runs must be stated in the mailing. No one may practice before that time.

C3 On any event using a practice lap just preceding the timed lap, there should be a turn just down course from the startline, such that cars must brake soon after crossing the startline. This is to eliminate any advantage an entrant might gain by avoiding gates or hitting markers on the practice lap, at no penalty, to cross the line at a higher speed.

C4 Sponsoring clubs must provide necessary safety equipment at all programs. Include one 10# (or larger) B or C class fire bottle (& other fire bottles as necessary), an adequate pry or crow bar, a broom, a PA system or megaphones, and crowd control devices.

C5 No visual or verbal instruction will be given to entrants during their timed competition except in emergencies or unless all entrants receive the instructions.

C6 "Fun-runs" or other use of the course & facilities set up for a Ch. Slalom, must be conducted only before or after timed runs with the same safety standards required at the *Ch. Slalom* (includes signing of a waiver).

C7 *Complete Results* shall be delivered to the series Scoring Chairman within 10 days of the event.

Results shall be mailed to all entrants within 30 days of the program (or A.S.A.P. following protest resolution if not resolved within time limits above). Results must include; *Driver* (name); *Vehicle* (make & model) & *class; Club affiliation* and notice of *Champ. driver registration; & net time for each event (run) with penalties noted.* Failure to do so will result in forfeiture for the "Event Of The Year".

C8 Championship Classes may not be modified for other than economic reasons. Then the only acceptable combinations are:

Stock (S)	*Race (R)*
Too few H/S-move to F/S or vice-versa	Too few F/R-move to E/R or vice-versa
Too few G/S-move to F/S	Too few F/R & E/R-move to B/R
Other "S" classes-move up	
Too few A/S-move to C/R	Other "R" classes-move up
	Too few A/R-move to M
	Too few M-run for FTD

Too few L-run in car's regular men's class

C9 Anyone pre-running the courses may not compete for points or trophies.

C10 The event chairman has the overall responsibility for the program of the day and is authorized to deal with the Stewards Committee & reject unsafe cars. He may disqualify anyone displaying unsafe or unsportsmanlike conduct only after a meeting with the Stewards Com.

C11 *Recommendation:* Members of the Stewards Committee should be present at each *Ch. Slalom* ½ hour before the first scheduled run and throughout the event. The course & administration should be checked in relation to the rules here stated; any recommendations on matters of safety & rules shall be made to the program chairman.

Section D Timing and Scoring Procedures

D1 Flying Start & Flying Finish will be used.

D2 If stopwatches are used, a primary and backup watch must be used at each course. All official watches at each course must be synchronized. Secondary timing equipment must be on hand, in case of failure of primary timing system.

D3 The method of starting, timing, judging, and scoring an event must remain constant throughout that event. Sufficient judges must be provided to adequately cover all parts of the course. All of these factors are subject to approval by the Sanction Committee, and review by the Stewards Committee.

D4 Run results should be displayed as soon as possible on a score board showing similar statistics as required on final results. (See Sect. C-7)

D5 Cars must be properly marked with a car number and class to provide quick identification by timing & course judges. Numbers should be at least 6″ high, with a 1″ stroke.

D6 Any driver who is flagged off or is forced to slow down for reasons beyond his control (includes timing malfunction), will be granted a *rerun*. Mechanical failures or driver error will not be considered as a reason for a rerun. (Recommendation: If a car DNF's for mechanical reasons on the first run, and is unable to return to competition, the driver may receive a refund of his entry fee at the discretion of the event chairman.)

D7 Three (3) seconds will be charged for each course marker (pylon) displaced by the vehicle, its accessories, or driver. Displacement - moving any part of a pylon out of its marked area. (See Sect. B-4)

D8 A *DNF* (Did Not Finish) will be charged for each of the following:

8-1 Each uncorrected deviation from the prescribed course. If the entrant corrects his error by completing the course correctly (from the point prior to the error), no penalty will be charged.

8-2 Driving with hands or arms outside of vehicle.

8-3 Failure to wear safety helmet or seatbelts.

8-4 Not having tonneau cover fully back from the front seat of a vehicle not equipped with a roll bar.

8-5 Displaying more than one set of numbers per side of car.

On items 8-2, 3, 4, 5 car is to be waved off course. It is recommended that a driver be told of course error, location, and incident as soon as possible.

D9 To score a DNF (on multi-course programs), the driver receives (for that run) the time of the slowest car in his class + 3 seconds.

Section E Scoring System For Championship Series

E1 Any member of a TSSCC affiliated club may register for participation in the Championship Slalom Series provided he/she is 18 years of age or over and possesses a valid driver's license.

E2 A driver meeting the above requirements, may register for the series at any time during the season. *Championship points will be awarded only for slaloms entered after registration procedures are completed with the Gym-Div Scoring Chairman.*

E3 The Championship Scoring system for *Men* will be printed in a supplement that will follow.

E4 The Championship Scoring system for *Ladies* is based on the time differential between lady's time and the 2nd fastest time of her car's respective men's class. The lowest time differential wins.

E5 A driver may enter only twice in any *Ch. Slalom.* Dual entries must further be in two different cars assigned to two different classes. Full entry fees will be paid for each, and both entries are eligible for full points, practice, and other privileges. Allowance of dual entries is, however, left to the discretion of the program chairman.

E6 A driver who competes in more than one class during the season will receive point credit for all points earned. To be eligible for a Championship award, a registered driver must have entered at least 50% of the *Ch. Slaloms* in that class.

E7 Championship awards will be made on the basis of the best 8 of the total number of slaloms entered in class. In case of a tie, the 8 will be advanced one program at a time until the tie is broken. This will affect only those involved in the tie. The number of Champ. awards will be determined by Gym-Div on the basis of the number of registrants earning points in each class and budget limitations.

E8 The Gym-Div Scoring Chairman will report current point standings at each Gym-Div meeting. He will furnish a list of current class standings to member representatives as often as changes are reported.

Section F Competitor Procedures and Eligibility

F1 Any given vehicle may be entered by no more than two drivers of the same sex, in a *Ch. Slalom,* for points and trophies.

F2 All drivers are required to wear Snell Foundation (or Z-90) approved safety helmets, and have seatbelts properly fastened while driving on course. Shatterproof eye protection is required in open cars with altered windshields.

F3 Unsafe and/or unsportsmanlike conduct by drivers at or near slalom location will be grounds for disqualification from that program.

F4 No driver under the influence of any alcoholic beverages or narcotics on the day of a *CH. SLA-*

LOM will be permitted to compete that day. No consumption of alcoholic beverages or narcotics are permitted at the site of a *CH. SLALOM.*

F5 While on course, drivers will keep their hands & arms inside vehicle under penalty of a red flag (immediate stop), and a DNF score for that run. (See other reasons for a DNF, Sect. D-8).

F6 No properly qualified registered driver may be turned away from an event because of over-crowding.

F7 A copy of these rules should be brought to each program by each registered driver.

Section G Car Preparation and Eligibility

G1 Only vehicles having a wheelbase of 75" or larger may compete on the *CH. SLALOM* Series.

G2 The use of locked or welded differentials is prohibited.

G3 All vehicles must pass a uniform tech inspection at each program. Entries must be refunded if a vehicle fails to pass. Standards of inspection will be high.

Mandatory Car Changes

G4 The following MUST be removed or accomplished *before* going thru tech - Steering wheel spinners; Spare tire, if not secured; Tools; Wheel covers; Unsecured floor mats; Side curtains, if not mounted; All loose items in driver's and trunk compartments. Passenger seat must be secured to prevent encumbrance to the driver.

G5 The Tonneau cover must be fully back from the front seat of a vehicle not equipped with a roll bar. Failure to comply will result in a DNF. (See Sect. D-8)

G6 Entrants must show identification numbers on *both* sides of car during all runs. Displaying more than one set of numbers will result in a DNF. (See Sect. D-8)

Optional Car Changes

G7 You MAY remove: Bumpers & brackets; Mufflers where allowed; Air cleaners; Rear seat, back or cushion (not both) and only if absolutely necessary for installation of an adequate roll bar.

G8 You MAY change or add to: Ignition systems; Springs; Shock absorbers; Anti-sway bars; Roll bars; Suspension, for safety and stability; Brakes.

Section H Class Definitions

H1 The class system is based on a schedule of *Stock (S), Racing (R), Modified (M), & Ladies (L)* classes. In the multi-class STOCK & RACING SCHEDULES, cars are classified on the basis of past and expected performance.

H2 A car may only run in the class for which it is prepared except as stated in the rules (Sect. C-8).

H3 Equipment or specifications may be exchanged between different years or models of a car IF: the years/models are in the same class, if the item is stock on the year/model from which it comes, the years and models have the same body-chassis specs (wheelbase, track, and suspension).

H4 The engine block and head(s) must be those specified by the manufacturer for that make and model car as original or replacement equipment for competition in S or R classes. Superchargers are allowed in R classes & only as factory part numbered options.

H5 *Stock (S)* - Cars eligible for competition in the Stock classes must be volume produced (100), and retain their original equipment and specs for the listed model of the car, with only the exceptions stated elsewhere in this code. If a specific model is not listed, then all normally available standard models are included.

    5-1 All models of a car are considered Stock with the equipment that makes up that model.

    5-2 Optional wheels are allowed, that do not

exceed stock dimensions or a ½″ alteration from stock track of that year/model, with a 7″ width maximum on F, G, & H class cars. Wheels must have standard diameter for that model.

5-3 Vehicle bodies must be stock, under the scrutiny of the Stewards Committee, to compete in Stock classes.

5-4 Tire must be completely under the fender (include sidewall), measured from the top of the wheel well.

H6 *Racing (R)* - Cars eligible for competition in Race classes are production cars, modified to improve performance (prodified) within the framework of this code. *Modifications moving Stock to Race class include:*

6-1 Using race designated or non-warranteed street tires.

6-2 Changing number or size of carbs or addition of fuel injection, unless allowed in Sect. H-3.

6-3 Using non-stock appearing modified intake or exhaust manifolding.

6-4 Updating or backdating if change affects class.

6-5 Flared fenders (must be done neatly); gutting interior; removing or substituting for glass; use of fiberglass panels, functioning as original permitted.

6-6 Tire crown must be under fender in Race class. Nonconforming cars will be moved to Mod. class.

H7 *Modified (M)* - All SCCA Sports/Racing cars, home & kit built cars (including engine swaps to different make or model not allowed in Sect. H-3). No tire, fender, or wheelbase modification limits, except minimum wheelbase of 75″.

H8 *Ladies (L)* - All lady entrants so specifying entry, may enter cars conforming to the preceding classing schedule. For scoring formula, see Sect. E-4.

H9 *Class Assignments for Makes & Models Listed Separately.*

Section I Protest Procedures

I1 TO PROTEST ANOTHER CAR: submit protest in writing, with $5 protest fee and the signature of another entrant in that class, to the event chairman, within 15 minutes of the protested car's last run. The protested car will submit to inspection by the program chairman & the Stewards Committee immediately. Failure to do so is considered admission of illegality. To this end, all *Ch. Slalom* entrants are asked to remain available at slalom site for 15 mins. after their final run. If the car is judged illegal the protest fee is returned to the protesting driver. If the car is judged legal the fee goes to the Champ. Award Fund. Burden of proof rests with the protestor, to be submitted in writing within 30 days, if the protest cannot be resolved on site. Sufficient notes and/or measurements will be taken to assure accurate resolution. Points earned before resolution of protest are held in suspension.

I2 Penalties for car illegality include: Loss of points for the Slalom in protest. A second upheld protest for the same reasons means loss of all Champ. standings for the season.

I3 *To Protest an Event:* submit protest in writing, with a $1 protest fee, within 15 minutes of the last competitive run. The protest must include the applicable section & rule number, the specific protest, and the desired action. A protest committee including the Stewards Committee and program chairman will meet on site to resolve the protest. Their decision will be announced within 45 min. after the protest is lodged.

I4 The Stewards Committee shall rule on all protests. In the event an equitable resolution of a protest cannot be made to one or both of the parties concerned, the matter can be brought before the Gym-Div Board, who will then either uphold the decision of the Stewards Committee or reopen the protest and have it reviewed at a joint meeting of the Stewards Committee and the Gym-Div Board. If the protest still remains unresolved, it will be brought up at an open and previously announced meeting of the Gym-Div body. A following majority vote will be declared as the decision, final & binding on all parties concerned.

1971 Tri-State Sports Car Conference Championship Slalom Car Classes

A/Stock (ltd. slip allowed)
Corvette (exc. L88 Engine)
Datsun 2000, 240-Z
Elva Courier 1800
Jaguar XKE
Lotus (all stock)
Morgan SS, +8
Porsche 911, Carrera, 914/6
Sunbeam Tiger
Triumph TR-5
Turner Ford
TVR 1800

B/Stock
Alfa 1600, 1750 Cpe/Rdstr.
Austin Healey 3000
BMW 1800TI, 2000TI, 2002
Cortina, Lotus (exc. BDA)
Datsun 1600 (rdstr.)
Elva Courier 1600
MGB, MGB-GT, MGC, MGC-GT
Morgan (exc. SS, +8)
Porsche 914/4, SC, S90

Saab Sonnett III
Triumph TR4, 4A, 250, 6

C/Stock
Alfa 1600, 1750
Austin Healey 100-4, 100-6, & Sprite 1275
BMW 1600, 1800, 2000
Capri 2000
Colt
Cortina GT
Datsun 1500 (rdstr.)
Fiat 124 Cpe. & Spider
Jaguar (pre XKE)
MG Midget 1275
Mini 1275 (exc. "S")
Opel 1900 GT
Pinto 2000
Porsche 912, 1500, 1600N, S,C
Saab Sonnett (exc. III)
Sunbeam Alpine (rdstr.)
Triumph GT6, 6+, Spitfire Mk3 & 4, TR2, 3, 3A, 3B
Vega 110 hp. (2 bbl.)

D/Stock
Alfa 1300 sedans & rdstrs.
Austin Healey Sprite 948
& 1100
Capri 1600
Cortina (all exc. in B&C)
Cricket
Datsun OHC sedans
Fiat 850 Spider
MGA, T series, Midget
948, & 1100
Mini 997, 1100 (exc. "S")
Opel 1900, & GT under
1900
Pinto 1600
Rover 2000
Toyota Mk II & OHC
Triumph Spitfire Mk 1, 2
Vega 90 hp. (1 bbl.)
Volvo 1800 series

E/Stock
Anglia
Austin America
Datsun Sedans (not in D)
Fiat sedans & 850 Cpe.
MG 1100, 1275 sedans
Mini 850
NSU 1200 TT (not TTS)
Opel (all exc. in C & D)
Renault (all exc. R8
Gordini)
Saab sedans
Sunbeam Imp
Toyota (all exc. in D)
Triumph sedans
Volvo (other than 1800)
VW (all)

F/Stock (ltd. slip allowed)
Sedans; 105" wheelbase
& over (incl. AMX —
Gremlin)
340 ci. & up w/hydro. lift.
260 ci. & up w/solid lift.
AMX over 290
Yenko Stinger

G/Stock (ltd. slip allowed)
Sedans; 105" wheelbase
& over (incl. AMX &
Gremlin)
339 ci. & under w/hydro.
lift.
259 ci. & under w/solid
lift.
AMX 290

H/Stock (ltd. slip allowed)
Sedans; 112" wheelbase &
over

L - All Ladies

A/Race
*Cobra
*Cortina BDA
Corvette, after 1963, L88
Engine (all)
*Griffith
Lotus Elan, +2, Europa, 7,
S7, etc.
Morgan SS, +8
Porsche 911, Carrera,
914/6
Turner Ford
*TVR Tuscan

---

*No stock class is allowed for this car

B/Race
*Alfa GTA (all)
Austin Healey 3000, 100-6
   and Sprite 1275
BMW 1600 and over
Cortina (Lotus only)
Corvette (prior to 1963)
Datsun 2000
Elva Courier 1600, 1800
*Fiat Abarth 1000, 1300
Jaguar (all)
MGB, MGB-GT, MGC,
   MGC-GT, and Midget
   1275
Mini 1275 and all "S"
Morgan (exc. SS, +8)
Porsche (all 4 cyl, exc.
   912)
Saab Sonnett (4 cyl. only)
Sunbeam Tiger
Triumph (all sports cars)

C/Race
Alfa (all exc. GTA)
Austin Healey 100-4 and
   Sprite 948, 1100
Cortina (all exc. Lotus)
Capri
Colt
Cricket
Datsun 1500, 1600 Sports
   & OHC Sedan
Fiat 124 Cpe. & Spider
MGA, T-series & Midget
   948, 1100
Mini 997, 1100 (exc. "S")
NSU TT
*NSU TTS

Opel GT
Pinto
Porsche 912
Rover 2000
Saab Sonnett (3 cyl. only)
Sunbeam Alpine (rdstr.)
Toyota Mk. II & OHC
Triumph 2000
Vega
Volvo 1800 series

D/Race
Anglia
Austin America
Datsun Sedans (exc. OHC)
Fiat (all exc. in B&C)
*Fiat Abarth 700, 850
MG 1100, 1275 Sedans
Mini 850
Opel (all exc. GT)
Renault (all incl. R8
   Gordini*)
Saab Sedans
Sunbeam Imp
Toyota (all exc. Mk II and
   OHC)
Triumph, Herald, TR-10
Volvo (all exc. 1800 series)
VW

E/Race
All 8 cyl. F, G, & H Stock
   Sedans

F/Race
All 6 cyl. F, G, & H Stock
   Sedans

*No stock class is allowed for this car

109

M-Modified

All SCCA open wheeled, Sports/Racing, Home Built and Kit cars (incl. engine swaps other than those noted in the rules)

SLALOM LOG

Use this log as a record of your performance during the year. Fill it in after every event. You'll be glad you have it next Winter when you can't remember how many slaloms you won.

Date	Event	Name	Sponsor Club	Location	Placing